Praise for

Designing *for* Excellence

"Laura's book is a must-read for every go-to-market leader. It's a sharp, operationally minded guide to enablement and sales productivity in an AI native world. Structured, technical, and grounded in real execution, it offers a clear blueprint for building processes and systems that scale. This isn't theory—it's a road map for what modern teams actually need in an AI world."

ELAY COHEN, CEO and cofounder of SalesHood

"It's rare to find someone who blends artistry and strategy with such finesse. From masterful culinary creations to a sharp, insightful take on enterprise sales enablement in the age of AI, Laura brings an unmatched depth of creativity and rigor. This book is a testament to her unique ability to distill complex ideas into actionable, human-centered wisdom. A must-read for anyone navigating the evolving landscape of sales—not fearing but embracing AI agents as selfless teammates."

DHEERAJ PANDEY, cofounder of Nutanix and DevRev

"At DevRev, we've seen firsthand how AI is reshaping the very foundation of go-to-market execution—and why enablement must evolve from a support layer into a system of performance. In this book, Laura Fu translates that shift with clarity, conviction, and hard-won insight. It's not just a framework for the future—it's a guide for building organizations that can learn, adapt, and scale with purpose. A powerful resource for any leader rethinking what great enablement looks like in an AI native world."

MANOJ AGARWAL, cofounder and president, DevRev

"In a world where sales motions are being redefined by AI, this book couldn't be more timely. Laura Fu offers a sharp, systems-level rethinking of enablement—not as a support function, but as the engine that turns strategy into action. Rather than cling to outdated playbooks, it presents a bold, product-driven approach grounded in human motivation, real-time orchestration, and continuous learning. For sales and enablement leaders, founders, and GTM operators navigating this shift, *Designing for Excellence* provides a critical framework for what comes next."

ITAMAR NOVICK, founder and general partner, Recursive Ventures

"*Designing for Excellence* is a powerful call to reimagine enablement— not as a support function, but as the operating system for modern GTM execution. Laura Fu brings clarity and structure to what many of us have felt: that behavior change, real-time orchestration, and intelligent systems are the new enablement frontier. At AdamX, we built our Synthetic Buyer platform to solve exactly the type of challenges Laura highlights—moving from episodic training to embedded, AI native workflows. It was an honor to be referenced in the book, but even more compelling to see how deeply aligned our philosophies are. This is essential reading for anyone building or evolving a revenue engine in today's AI-driven world."

NEEL KAMAL, founder and CEO, AdamX

"Laura Fu is a triple threat and a true force of nature across sales strategy, execution, and operations. Her insights on where the future of GTM and RevOps are headed in the era of AI are gold!"

JUSTIN VANDEHEY, CEO and cofounder of Thread

"For any founder, operator, or GTM leader navigating go-to-market execution in the AI era, this book is indispensable. Laura Fu provides the clear, actionable blueprint for building the intelligent, orchestrated systems required to win in today's market."

PATRICK SALYER, partner, Mayfield

Designing *for* Excellence

Designing

for

Excellence

Sales Enablement in
the AI Native World

Laura Fu

amplify
an imprint of Amplify Publishing Group

amplify

an imprint of Amplify Publishing Group

www.amplifypublishinggroup.com

Designing for Excellence: Sales Enablement in the AI Native World

For more information, please contact:
Amplify Publishing, an imprint of Amplify Publishing Group
620 Herndon Parkway, Suite 220
Herndon, VA 20170
info@amplifypublishing.com

Library of Congress Control Number: 2025916998

CPSIA Code: PRV0925A

ISBN-13: 979-8-89138-908-3

Printed in the United States

For my children, who have taught me what true enablement looks like in growth, grace, perseverance, and leadership.

CONTENTS

The Beginnings

This journey didn't begin in a classroom or a corporate training department. It started in the kitchen.

As a classically trained chef working in Michelin-star kitchens, I learned how to lead under pressure, systematize execution, and build experiences that were precise, repeatable, and personal. What I loved most wasn't the food. It was the orchestration. The pressure. The rhythm. The way a team came together around a common goal and delivered with care and clarity. That mindset shaped how I lead to this day.

When I transitioned into tech, enablement wasn't part of my title. However, it quickly became part of my job. Each time I built a new team, scaled a function, or launched a market, there it was again: the need to enable people. No playbooks. No onboarding systems. Just a group of people trying to find their footing in a fast-moving environment. And so, piece by piece, I started designing the systems I wished I'd had.

Those early enablement sessions happened in my garage. In true startup fashion, I flew my team in, set up folding chairs, and led sessions packed with live exercises, real deals, and open dialogue. At night, I cooked dinner for everyone. It was scrappy. It was personal. And it worked. That's when I saw it clearly: enablement isn't about polish. It's about connection, intention, and context that actually lands.

Later, while launching a managed services business, one of my top priorities was building a global partner network. That meant enabling Big Four consultants—people with limited time and high expectations. Over three-day sessions, I had to design a program to keep them engaged and learning. That's where I leaned into motivation and gamification. I created a simple system: answer a question well, earn a branded pin; trade pins for prizes. It felt playful, but it worked. The room lit up. And I was reminded that people don't just want to learn—they want to *win*.

Then came Japan.

Sprinklr was expanding into the Japanese market through partners, and I was tasked with enabling a group of thirty partner sellers as our first Go-To-Market team. Every word had to go through a translator. Every message had to be simplified. The experience sharpened my instincts for clarity. What mattered wasn't the tech-forward vocabulary. It was salience. What stuck. What resonated. The experience taught me that great enablement travels across language and culture when it's grounded in simplicity and purpose.

Eventually, my journey led me to the CRO's office, supporting broader go-to-market execution. We were analyzing performance gaps across segments, regions, and tenures. And one insight kept surfacing: Rep productivity was being dragged down by fragmented onboarding and inconsistent ongoing training. Enablement had gone from a tactical patch to a strategic imperative.

That's how I stepped into my first formal enablement role, leading a team and designing programs at scale. And here's where my non-L&D background became an unexpected strength.

Rather than approaching it like a curriculum designer, I thought like a field operator. I asked myself: *What would I want if I were a rep?* Not a firehose of information—just enough to be dangerous. Something digestible. Actionable. Something that respects your time and still gets results. That mindset became the foundation of my program design: prioritize clarity, minimize fluff, and build just enough structure to support performance without getting in the way.

All throughout, I was fortunate to learn from some of the best. I worked with Dick Dunkel, the founder of MEDDPICC. I absorbed the principles of Force Management. I learned from leaders who came out of PTC and codified what sales excellence and consistency look like at scale. That season of immersion taught me how to bring rigor to intuition—how to measure enablement in ways that mattered to the business, not just the learner.

But the most profound influence on my approach hasn't come from work. It has come from home.

Becoming a mom transformed how I teach, lead, and learn. It forced me to slow down. To simplify. To meet people where they are. I learned that everyone absorbs differently. And that success isn't about how well *I* explain something, but how clearly *they* understand it. When something doesn't land, the answer isn't to double down. It's to reframe, try again, and stay patient.

That mindset of graceful persistence became the most important tool in my enablement toolkit. It's how I approach every workshop, every rollout, every feedback loop. Enablement isn't about proving how much you know. It's about being useful to the other person, again and again.

Today, I think of myself as a lifelong enabler. Whether I'm guiding a team through a product launch, mentoring a new hire, or helping one of my kids with a tough question, the goal is the same: to leave them more confident, capable, and grounded than when we began.

They say to teach is to change a life. I've been lucky to change a few, and even luckier to be changed in the process.

Becoming an enabler wasn't part of the plan. But in hindsight, I was doing it all along. In kitchens, in garages, across cultures and teams. What started as instinct became intention. What started as chaos became clarity. And what started as a side responsibility became the work I love most.

This book is a reflection of that journey. Of the people I've taught. The people who have taught me. The systems I've built, broken, and rebuilt again. It's not about perfection—it's about finding what works well enough to help someone grow.

Introduction

Sales enablement has become one of the most discussed—and often misunderstood—functions in modern go-to-market organizations. Depending on who you ask, it's a training team, a content function, a support layer, or something in between.

But the truth is, enablement has always been more than that. It's not a deliverable; it's a system, one that, when built well, drives behavior change at scale, reinforces execution, and connects field motion directly to business outcomes.

That system might include tools, training, coaching, content, data, or analytics—but enablement itself isn't defined by any single component. What matters is how those parts come together to shape performance. Enablement isn't just what's delivered. It's how consistently learning, insight, and action reach the field.

Now, as AI reshapes the way we learn, decide, and work, enablement is entering a new chapter.

There's excitement—new tools, new workflows, and the promise of personalization at scale. But there's also confusion. Because if the system behind it all is still fragmented, episodic, or reactive, AI won't transform it. It will simply accelerate the gaps.

This book isn't about AI in theory. It's about what AI *requires* in practice.

This book explores how AI native tools—across coaching, enrichment, sequencing, analytics, and orchestration—are reshaping the way enablement is delivered. But those technologies only succeed when paired with the right foundations: clarity, shared ownership, and system design.

That's why this book begins with the enduring principles of great enablement and then shows how AI changes the speed, structure, and scale of every part of the system.

Some of what's described is already in use. Some is aspirational by design. This book is not just a playbook for what to implement today. It's a blueprint for what to build next. The tools may still be evolving, but the architecture and mindset are within reach. The goal is to help operators and builders close that gap—faster, smarter, and more aligned to how performance actually happens.

Here's how the book is structured:

- **Section 1: Purpose and Principles**
  The five core principles that define effective enablement—relevant with or without AI
- **Section 2: Metrics That Matter**
  A shift from lagging performance metrics to leading behavioral indicators and system health
- **Section 3: The Enablement Flywheel**
  A new model for ongoing, real-time enablement fueled by AI and delivered through coaching, content, and tooling in sync
- **Section 4: What's Needed to Get There**
  The architectural, organizational, and cultural shifts required to move from programs to platforms.

Whether you're a sales leader, an enablement practitioner, a RevOps strategist, or a platform builder, this book is for those on the hook for execution—people designing the systems, leading the teams, or shaping the motions that drive revenue. The goal is to give you the language, structure, and clarity to lead differently. Not just to react to change but to shape it. Not just to keep up but to build a system that moves ahead of it.

This isn't about adding AI to enablement. It's about redesigning enablement so that it scales, adapts, and thrives in a world where motion is constant and expectations are higher than ever.

Let's reimagine what enablement can be—starting with what good looks like.

📖 *What We Mean by "AI Native"*

In this book, "AI native" refers to systems designed for the current era of AI—built on infrastructure that supports large-scale data, real-time reasoning, and autonomous action. These systems don't just incorporate AI features; they treat intelligence as the foundation.

1

Guiding Principles of Sales Enablement

Regardless of whether AI is part of the picture, great enablement has always been about building systems that drive real behavior change at scale, align tightly to business outcomes, and empower both reps and managers to succeed.

This section outlines the five core principles that sit at the heart of any high-performing enablement strategy. These aren't just reactions to the rise of AI—they're fundamentals that apply in any era. But as our tools become more intelligent and our workflows more dynamic, these principles become even more essential. They guide us in building systems that aren't just technically sophisticated but truly human-centered—designed to help people learn, apply, and perform.

1.1 Enablement Drives Performance Through Systems, Not Individuals

Enablement is a system that drives results by coordinating people, programs, and platforms around field productivity. But systems don't build themselves. Great enablement requires investment and cross-functional partnership. True enablement success requires alignment and active collaboration across the entire company.

Key business partners include the following:

- Sales Leadership—to reinforce accountability and coaching
- Revenue Operations—to bring in metrics, capacity modeling, and inspection
- Product Marketing—to deliver consistent positioning and messaging that maps to customer value

- Product and Engineering—to keep the field informed of roadmap evolution and new capabilities
- Customer Success—to align on adoption, renewals, and feedback loops from the post-sales journey

Enablement systems also span a range of capabilities that support behavior change and execution. These might include the following:

- Call coaching—to support skill development through real rep conversations
- Sales engagement—to drive outreach consistency and measure pipeline generation efforts
- Content enablement—to ensure reps have access to the right message at the right time
- Learning delivery and tracking—to measure progress across onboarding and development

- Productivity insights and analytics—to surface behavior trends and flag early risks

This integrated approach ensures enablement is embedded throughout the customer lifecycle and sales process, not siloed as a training function.

Too often, enablement is treated as an individual role or reactive resource—someone brought in to deliver a training, update a deck, or fix an immediate problem. But when enablement is framed this way, it becomes disconnected from the broader system—and worse, it becomes a single point of failure. It assumes that one individual can curate, synthesize, and deliver everything a seller needs to know to drive the company's growth. That's an impossible burden, not only because of the sheer volume of information but because it reinforces a model where enablement is expected to operate in isolation. Eventually, programs are launched without reinforcement, messaging gets lost between functions, and behavior change struggles to stick.

A shared approach to enablement solves for this by distributing ownership across teams and connecting enablement to the levers that actually drive performance, like frontline coaching, deal inspection, and tool engagement. With the right structure and support, enablement evolves from reactive function to strategic driver. It becomes a muscle that builds over time—reinforced by shared priorities, sustained through cross-functional habits, and measured by its impact on execution.

About the Field Notes: All of the field notes in this book are drawn from programs I've led, spanning startups, scale-ups, and global go-to-market teams. They're not case studies but snapshots, real-world examples of enablement principles in motion. Each one is included to illustrate how the ideas in that section play out in practice—sometimes in full, sometimes in part, but always in the field.

Field Note: Operationalizing Account Planning Across Go-To-Market (GTM)

When we rolled out account planning as a discipline across the entire GTM team, we didn't treat it as a sales-only initiative. We built it as a cross-functional muscle. Each section of the account plan was designed with a specific functional contributor in mind—SDRs, AEs,

CSMs, product, even marketing. This allowed us to map the customer's business holistically and tie opportunity to everything from unmet needs to upcoming product releases.

Building account planning as a shared muscle didn't just mean creating a new template; it required changes across coaching, collaboration, and leadership inspection. We trained teams by role, embedded examples in deal reviews, and aligned leaders to model it consistently. The result wasn't just better documentation—it was better teamwork. Over time, the system took hold. The mindset shifted. And with it, 65 percent of new business came from existing customers.

📕 *What We Mean by "Account Planning"*

Account planning is the process of aligning your team around how to engage, grow, and support a key account. It includes identifying stakeholders, understanding business objectives, mapping pain points, and sequencing actions across sales, product, support, and marketing. In the best execution of this, account planning is not a static template.

> *It is a living system that adjusts based on signals, prioritizes focus, and helps teams act in sync.*

1.2 Enablement Requires Motivation and Reinforcement

Motivation and inspiration are the starting points of enablement. Reps must first connect emotionally and intellectually to the "why" behind what they're learning; this creates the commitment needed to follow through. But motivation isn't a one-time spark—it must be reinforced daily. Managers play a vital role in keeping that motivation alive through praise, deal support, and vision setting. Peer-driven energy through team huddles, story sharing, and collaborative sessions also reinforces belief.

But motivation alone isn't enough. It must be continually nurtured and reinforced. Reps have to believe they can succeed, and that belief needs to be protected and strengthened over time. Whether it's through celebrating small wins, surfacing exciting product developments, or simply seeing their name at the top of a leaderboard, motivation must be sustained by inspiration.

On the flip side, when reinforcement exists but motivation is absent, reps disengage. You can have every system in place—content libraries, training cadences, call coaching—but if reps don't believe in the mission or see a path to success, nothing sticks. No one internalizes a playbook when they feel defeated. No one adopts new messaging when they're being hounded, not helped. When enablement turns into a checklist—generic sessions, forced messaging, or one-size-fits-all delivery—the spark fades.

To drive real change, reinforcement must follow motivation, and motivation must be intentional. It should be embedded into how leaders communicate, how programs are positioned, and how reps are recognized. Sales plays shouldn't live in a single deck—they should show up consistently across the enablement journey. Reinforcement is most powerful when inspiration is embedded in every format: Onboarding should spark belief in what's possible, instructor-led training (ILT) should energize through role-plays and peer interaction, and modules should remind reps why the content matters. Whether it's manager 1:1s, call reviews, or team huddles, every touchpoint should reinforce not just what to do but why it's worth doing.

Enablement is a rhythm powered by belief, reinforced through behavior, and sustained through systems that motivate and support the field. Managers are the amplifiers, but reps have to be the believers. Without both, the rhythm breaks. Motivation must be felt, and reinforcement must be seen.

📕 *What We Mean by "Sales Plays"*

A sales play is a repeatable motion designed to drive a specific outcome, such as landing a new customer, expanding within an existing account, or accelerating deal velocity. Each play includes recommended messaging, content, tools, and next steps tailored to that goal. Sales plays work best when they are adaptable to real deal context rather than being static checklist.

⫰ Field Note: Fueling Motivation Through Recognition

One consistent method used to reinforce motivation has been the Pipeline Generation (PG) Race, a weekly program rolled out across multiple organizations. Each week, reps are ranked on activity-based metrics such as discovery calls, pipeline created, and opportunity generation. The results are shared in a leaderboard-style email distributed to sales leadership and executive staff.

Although the program wasn't focused on closing business, reps consistently felt energized by the visibility of their names "on the board"—especially when recognized at the highest levels. Some weeks offered team prizes; others had no prizes at all. Still, the recognition itself became a source of motivation.

Over time, the PG Race helped shift the perception of pipeline creation from a behind-the-scenes metric to a celebrated milestone. It demonstrated that pipeline motion wasn't just about activities—it was about momentum. By spotlighting early-stage wins, the program helped reinforce that building pipeline is just as valuable as closing it.

📓 *What We Mean by "Pipeline Generation" (PG)*

Pipeline generation refers to the set of seller-led activities required to create new sales opportunities. This includes outbound prospecting, discovery calls, and proactive engagement across target accounts.

*Some businesses operate in **demand-fulfillment** environments where brand recognition, mature categories, or inbound volume drive consistent opportunity flow. In contrast, for **PG businesses**, especially those selling new, technical, or category-defining products (like AI), there is no built-in demand. Reps must create it.*

In these settings, pipeline isn't captured. It's built. That means early sales behaviors like outreach, narrative framing, and education are not just helpful; they're existential. As a result, many pipeline generation businesses treat created pipeline as the most reliable and healthy leading indicator of performance.

1.3 Sales Reps Deserve Clarity, Which Brings Confidence

Sales teams operate in an environment of constant information flow—new content, shifting priorities, changing plays. Effective enablement doesn't just reduce noise; it adds meaningful signal. Enablement should deliver a clear, consistent message that resonates with what matters to reps in the context of their current deals, targets, and priorities. That means reps should always know:

- What matters right now: What should I be focusing on this week?
- Where to find it: Is it in the learning management system (LMS), the customer relationship management platform (CRM), or a shared Slack channel?
- How it connects: How does this content relate to the current play, campaign, or sales priority?
- What's in it for me: How does this help me hit my number or solve a current challenge in my deals?

Great enablement is thematic and sequenced. It connects the dots across onboarding, ongoing development, and deal execution. When initiatives are rolled out with intention and coherence, reps can absorb and apply what they learn.

But when clarity is missing, even the most well-designed programs fall flat. Reps may struggle to understand how a new message or play fits into their priorities or how to apply it using the frameworks they've been taught. They may be unsure of the next steps in a rollout or hesitant to introduce something new—like a product feature or campaign—because they don't know how to position it, where it fits, or what happens after.

Instead of feeling equipped, they feel uncertain or overwhelmed. The business may assume reps were enabled, but without clarity, nothing sticks.

Enablement should also provide reps with the clarity and depth needed to build confidence—not only in delivering the message but in owning the conversation that follows. Confidence comes from knowing what to say and how to respond. While iteration is expected in fast-paced environments, half-baked rollouts can erode trust. When reps face customer questions like

"How much does it cost?" or "What does implementation look like?", they need to feel ready, not uncertain. Great enablement anticipates these follow-on moments and equips reps with guidance, messaging, and example responses that boost confidence under pressure. Clarity isn't just about knowing the content. It's about being confident enough to use it in the moment.

✒ Field Note: Creating Context Before Content

When launching a new product, the team began by aligning internally on three foundational questions:

- Why are we doing this?
- Why is now the right time?
- Why is this the right product for the market?

From there, reps were provided with a clear, compelling narrative that explained the broader industry landscape, the market opportunity, and why the product mattered to the customer. It was, effectively, a prelaunch internal pitch, focused not on product specs but on building belief and contextual understanding.

Only after that foundation was established did the enablement team move into product details. As a result, reps understood not only what the product did but why it mattered—how it would help their customers, their company, and their own pipeline. That clarity anchored the message so reps not only understood what to say but why it mattered, and they felt ready to lead customer conversations from day one.

1.4 Design for Action, Not Just Information Transfer

Great enablement doesn't just inform—it equips. Sales reps need content that helps them understand the "why" behind a message, the "how" to apply it, and the confidence to take action in live customer conversations. To make this possible, enablement must be designed with field application in mind. Learning takes multiple touches. It's not just about telling someone once; it's about repetition and reinforcement across channels and moments. Reps need to read it, hear it, practice it, get it wrong, try again, and eventually apply it in real conversations. That's what good enablement design looks like: deliberate, multi-touch, and iterative.

Use consistent frameworks (like the 3 Whys and Command of the Message®)* to give reps a familiar, repeatable structure. Familiarity builds confidence. When reps encounter consistent frameworks across different trainings, they're better able to internalize, recall, and apply that knowledge. Repetition in structure accelerates learning, reduces confusion, and creates fluency in how reps approach conversations, regardless of topic or format.

Design content to be progressive and digestible by distilling what's essential and sequencing concepts in a logical microlearning format. Reps should be able to build understanding in small, cumulative steps that reinforce each other rather than be overwhelmed by large one-time information drops.

---

* Command of the Message® is a trademark of Force Management. This book references the concept, not the proprietary training.

📔 *What We Mean by "Microlearning"*

Microlearning refers to short, focused lessons designed to be consumed in small bursts. In sales enablement, it means delivering content in a way that reinforces core ideas through repetition and builds understanding over time. The goal isn't to cover everything at once but to help reps absorb and apply information at the pace of real work.

Examples include a three-minute video walking through objection handling for a specific persona, a Slack-based call review prompt that highlights one behavior to watch for, or a deal review moment where a manager reinforces a key play.

Tie enablement to real selling moments using call scenarios, objection handling, and in-deal examples to drive relevance. The most impactful content doesn't come from a slide. It comes from the field. Build enablement based on real customer interactions, rep feedback, and winning conversations. Collaborate with frontline managers and top performers to validate what actually works. When reps recognize their voice in the material, they're more likely to trust it—and use it. The best enablement content is built from proven success stories, customer conversations, and frontline feedback. This ensures that messaging is grounded in credibility, resonates with the reality of selling, and is adaptable to the follow-on questions that reps actually hear. Leverage insights from the field to ground enablement in authenticity, credibility, and proven success.

Encourage reflection and practice so reps aren't just exposed to ideas but actually apply them. When enablement focuses only on information transfer—checklist trainings, long slide decks, or product overviews—it creates surface-level awareness without field impact. Reps may remember what was taught, but they don't know when to use it, how to adapt it, or why it matters now. Content that isn't actionable becomes background noise. And when reps can't apply what they've learned, the business assumes they weren't paying attention when in reality, the enablement wasn't built for behavior change.

True enablement doesn't stop at delivery. It requires opportunities for reps to test, rehearse, and refine their understanding. This means building in role-plays, field exercises, and mock customer scenarios as standard parts of enablement programming. Enablement must be seen not as a point-in-time activity but as an ongoing rhythm of learning, doing, and adjusting based on what's working in the field.

Learning without application doesn't drive outcomes. Effective enablement bridges the gap between knowledge and action by giving reps multiple opportunities to internalize and apply what they've learned. This also means understanding that content for customers is different from content for sales. While marketing assets are designed to persuade buyers, sales enablement content must help reps understand and explain the product. It should simplify complex ideas, anticipate follow-up questions, and give reps the language to position value clearly. Great sales content isn't polished—it's practical. It's designed to be understood quickly, remembered easily, and used naturally in conversations with real customers.

🖊 Field Note: Sequencing Skills by Stage

In one onboarding program, we made a deliberate decision to teach new reps only the first two stages of the sales process, which were focused solely on pipeline generation. We didn't introduce later-stage concepts like negotiation or closing because those moments weren't relevant yet.

This decision ran counter to some expectations; we weren't covering the full playbook. But the goal wasn't to be exhaustive. It was to be effective. By narrowing scope, we helped new reps focus on the motions that mattered most—creating opportunities. This allowed them to enter a rhythm of learning, doing, and adjusting early in their journey. Instead of overwhelming them with the full playbook, we built fluency through focused repetition. Once they had confidence and traction at the top of the funnel, we layered in later-stage concepts at the moment they became relevant, about three to four months later.

📖 What We Mean by "Sales Process" and "Sales Stages"

The sales process is the structured set of steps a company uses to move a buyer from initial engagement to closed revenue. These steps are typically broken into sales stages, such as Discover, Qualify, Evaluate, Validate, Negotiate, and Close.

Each stage reflects a different part of the customer journey and requires different behaviors, messaging, and tools. In effective enablement, training and content are mapped to where a rep actually is in the process—especially during onboarding, where early-stage skills like outreach and discovery matter more than late-stage motions like negotiation.

1.5 Rep Development Is Owned by Managers, Supported by Enablement

Enablement plays a powerful supporting role in sales performance. It serves as the launching pad that equips reps with the knowledge, tools, and frameworks they need to succeed. While it lays the foundation and structure, it cannot replace the daily coaching, account-ability, and performance management that only front-line managers can deliver.

True rep development is a shared system of ownership.

Managers own performance. They are closest to the rep's behaviors and responsible for reinforcing expecta-tions, delivering feedback, and driving improvement.

Enablement owns the environment. It provides the tools, frameworks, knowledge, and training that give managers and reps the foundation to succeed. These resources also serve as a critical resource for managers to leverage, offering support in coaching preparation, surfacing skill gaps, and reinforcing key behaviors. When managers lean on enablement as a partner, they're better equipped to drive consistent development across their teams.

When this system breaks—when managers depri-oritize coaching or reps disengage from their own growth—development stalls. Enablement may still deliver high-quality programs, but without consistent follow-through from managers, even the best training fades. Reps start to treat enablement as a checkbox, and managers shift into reactive mode, focused only on lagging performance instead of building future capability. When spot coaching replaces skill building, growth becomes unpredictable.

Reps own their development. They must engage with the content, seek feedback, and apply what they've learned to real-world situations. Historically, enablement has shown a strong correlation with top-performing reps; they tend to engage more deeply with enablement, absorb the material, and apply it consistently. However, enablement alone is not the cause of performance. It amplifies the effort of high performers, but it cannot replace the need for personal ownership or effective management. This underscores why development must be shared—reps, managers, and enablement each play a different role in turning learning into outcomes.

One of the most effective ways to bring this to life is through structured skill/will assessments used by AEs and managers for a consistent rhythm of development. This should give managers a shared language for evaluating rep behaviors, spotting gaps, and tailoring coaching accordingly while helping reps understand what good looks like and where they stand. Enablement can support this system by creating the framework, aligning it to daily workflows, and equipping managers to use it during 1:1s.

📓 What We Mean by "Skill and Will"

The skill/will framework helps managers assess where a rep stands based on two dimensions of performance:

__Skill__ is demonstrated capability. It shows up in execution and lagging indicators like win rate, conversion, or deal velocity.

__Will__ is day-to-day behavior. It shows up in leading indicators like effort, consistency, and engagement, even if outcomes haven't landed yet.

This distinction helps managers diagnose the root of a performance gap. A rep with high will but low skill may be doing the right things, just not doing them well yet. A rep with high skill but low will may be capable but disengaged or misaligned. Framing performance through both lenses enables more targeted coaching and support.

✒ Field Note: Building a Shared Language for Coaching

We implemented a skill/will performance rubric to guide SDR development across the team. The framework defined nine skill areas—from discovery to stakeholder engagement to operational excellence—each with clear definitions, observable behaviors, and coaching guidance.

Managers used this framework during 1:1s to identify gaps and create action plans. Reps began self-assessing and tracking progress, which gave them clarity and ownership. Enablement supported the rollout with manager training, use case examples, and templates. What started as a tool became a rhythm integrated into weekly inspection, performance reviews, and even hiring.

See Exhibit A:
SDR Skill/Will Performance Assessment

Enablement works best when it integrates into this rhythm of inspection, coaching, and application, not as a replacement for it. A rep's success doesn't rest with one function—it depends on alignment and consistency across all three. Enablement should be judged not only by engagement but by how effectively it supports this shared system of development.

Ultimately, the impact of enablement must be seen in business outcomes—pipeline created, deals progressed, revenue won. But to influence these outcomes, we must first understand the behaviors that predict them. That's where we'll begin in the next section.

2

Core Outcomes
and Metrics

Enablement is successful when it drives measurable, lasting behaviors that improve field performance. These behaviors—when clearly defined, tracked, and reinforced—become the leading indicators that predict whether performance will follow. In this section, we'll explore how to define, measure, and apply these metrics across ramping (those still within their onboarding window) and ramped reps (those past it, based on time, even if true productivity varies). Sales performance is defined as attainment against quota and other revenue outcomes. These are lagging indicators, and while enablement contributes, it is not the sole driver.

While sales performance (e.g., quota attainment, win rate, revenue contribution) is the ultimate outcome, it cannot be the sole measure of enablement impact. Sales performance is influenced by many factors outside the scope of enablement, territory quality, product maturity, pricing, and market timing among them. As a result, we focus on productivity metrics—those that reflect the rep's ability to execute key behaviors that precede performance. These are more directly shaped by enablement programs, easier to observe and measure in real time, and provide early insight into whether the right motions are taking place. Productivity is based on the specific field behaviors that an organization defines as predictors of success and will vary by company depending on sales motion, deal cycle, and GTM strategy.

Sales productivity is defined as the consistent generation of qualified pipeline and the effective progression of deals through the funnel. It's the leading indicator of performance and the earliest sign that enablement is landing. These behaviors are intentionally selected and agreed upon by the leadership team as the best available hypothesis for what predicts future performance. Because they are observable, coachable, and repeatable, they allow the business to course correct earlier than lagging indicators like win rate or quota attainment.

2.1 Understanding Ramp and Time to Productivity

Ramp is measured in time, but time to productivity is about behavior. A rep may be ramped based on time since hire but still unproductive if they haven't demonstrated consistent field activity or pipeline contribution.

- Time to Ramp: How long it takes a new hire to complete onboarding milestones (typically tracked in months)
- Time to Productivity: How quickly a rep reaches benchmarks such as number of discovery calls, new business meetings, and created pipeline. These activities were selected not because they guarantee success but because they are early, observable behaviors that historically correlate with long-term

performance. Unlike win rates or revenue, which lag, these activities give us real-time visibility into rep motion and allow for earlier coaching and course correction.

Enablement's role is to accelerate both, getting reps to milestone completion *and* activating meaningful motion in the field. But momentum fades quickly without manager reinforcement. Even highly motivated reps can stall without timely support. As outlined in the principle Enablement Requires Motivation and Reinforcement, it's not enough to deliver a program. Reps need consistent coaching and encouragement to translate learning into sustained behavior.

To operationalize this distinction, a different set of metrics should be used to track early and ongoing behaviors that signal whether reps are in motion and trending toward performance. The leading indicators give managers and enablement teams a shared real-time view of rep activity. This makes it possible to spot momentum, identify risk, and course correct before issues show up in lagging outcomes like win rate or revenue.

Key leading indicators include:

- Pipeline Coverage: Percentage of reps at or above target coverage for the next quarter and next-plus-one quarter (NQ, NQ+1)

📕 What We Mean by "Pipeline Coverage"

Pipeline coverage refers to the ratio of open pipeline to quota, typically measured for future quarters. For example, a rep with $1.5M in qualified pipeline for a $500K quarterly target has 3x coverage.

Many teams use 3–4x as a common benchmark, but coverage needs vary depending on segment, region, sales cycle, and whether the business is driven by new or existing accounts. The most accurate view comes from looking at consistency across peer groups, such as new business reps in the same region or stage. In the absence of this granularity, overall coverage is still a useful signal for early risk detection, especially when tracked at both the next quarter (NQ) and the next-plus-one (NQ+1).

- Pipeline Generation Activity: Volume and consistency of discovery calls, new business meetings, and created pipeline
- Sales Play Adoption: Frequency and consistency with which reps apply specific sales plays (measured via CRM tagging, call analysis, asset usage, and manager inspection)

2.2 Ramping Metrics and Progressive Expectations

For new hires, productivity targets are staged intentionally by month. Early in a rep's ramp, expectations are lighter to allow time for learning, shadowing, and foundational skill building. As reps progress, expectations increase incrementally toward full productivity. This approach helps:

- Build confidence without overwhelming new reps;
- Align developmental milestones with observed behavior; and
- Identify early signals of engagement and coachability.

This approach is also a reflection of the broader enablement design principle: design content to be progressive and digestible. Rather than overwhelming new hires with everything at once, we embrace a microlearning approach, sequencing concepts and behaviors so reps build confidence and capability in manageable stages.

Ramping AE Productivity Benchmarks (Sample)

Month	Discovery Calls	New Business Meetings	Go/No-Go Decisions	Created Pipeline
1	5	0	0	$0
2	10	2	0	$40K
3	20	4	1	$120K
4	30	8	3	$275K
5	35	13	5	$450K

Fully Ramped AE Productivity Benchmarks (Quarterly Targets)

Metric	Quarterly Target
Discovery Calls	30
New Business Meetings	10
Go/No-Go Decisions	5
Created Pipeline	$800K

⧦ Field Note: Early Activity Wins, But Watch What Happens Next

Here's what we found: After introducing these new ramping metrics with benchmarks by time in seat (see table Ramping AE Productivity Benchmarks above), newly hired AEs began executing pipeline generation activity significantly earlier. Within two quarters of the program's rollout, we saw new reps engaging in meaningful discovery and meeting generation within their first two months—well ahead of the prior baseline of three months or more.

The system successfully accelerated early motion, but without continued guidance, the reps' development curve dipped. Because all focus was placed on the first six months of onboarding, there was little support for the transition into later-stage execution. As a result, close rates for these newly ramped reps dropped from 85 percent to 70 percent in their third quarter.

The takeaway: Early activity metrics work, so keep them. But the real risk isn't during ramp—it's right after. Development doesn't end at month six. It evolves.

2.3 Enablement Program Engagement Metrics

While enablement should always be eventually measured by business outcomes, there are leading indicators that tell us how thoughtfully enablement programs are designed, delivered, and consumed. These metrics reflect what enablement can directly control: the field's consumption of and engagement with its programs. They indicate whether programs are practical, creatively delivered, and valuable to the field, and they help identify where to reinforce success or make improvements.

Leading indicators of program engagement include the following:

- Program attendance: Percentage of reps participating in live or virtual enablement sessions
- Completion rates: Percentage of reps completing required training or onboarding tracks
- Knowledge checks or assessments: Scores or pass rates on quizzes tied to key concepts
- Content engagement: Views, shares, or time spent on recorded training, documents, or enablement tools
- Manager inspection: How often managers are coaching to or referencing enablement in 1:1s or deal reviews

While these signals are not enough on their own, they provide early feedback on whether enablement is being received and retained, which is the necessary foundation for behavior change in the field.

Field Note: What the Best Reps Taught Us About Enablement Consumption

The relationship between sales enablement and sales performance is often assumed to be linear, but in practice, it's more nuanced.

We found that top-performing reps typically engaged with around 50 percent of available enablement programs and content. But it wasn't about volume—it was about intent. These reps knew where their gaps were and chose the most relevant resources to support execution in the field. They didn't consume everything; they consumed strategically.

Interestingly, we also saw that reps who consumed more enablement but lacked strong frontline coaching often struggled to translate learning into action. Instead of spending time in the field, they stayed in the "lab," treating enablement as a substitute for selling rather than a support system. And for disengaged reps with low motivation, no amount of content made up for the absence of accountability and drive.

This insight doesn't devalue enablement. It reframes how we measure its impact. In any system, not all resources will be used equally. That's not a failure of design. It's a reflection of maturity. The goal isn't universal consumption; it's targeted application. The system should be built to support intentional engagement: manager-guided, context-aware, and tailored to the rep's needs in real time.

The best reps used enablement as a lever, not a lifeline, and they were supported by systems that helped them apply learning with precision.

Metrics tell us what matters. But to change those metrics, we need enablement systems that shape rep behavior daily—in context, in the field, and in motion. This is where the enablement flywheel comes in, not just as a delivery model but a performance engine that connects content, programs, tools, and analytics into a continuous loop of learning and execution.

3

The Enablement
Flywheel

The ideal state of enablement is one that continuously delivers insight, guidance, and feedback to the field—on time, in context, and at scale. When enablement functions as a closed loop, it reinforces key behaviors, accelerates ramp, and allows the business to adapt quickly to what's working.

Historically, enablement strategies have been too static. Programs were delivered once, content went stale, and feedback loops were weak or nonexistent. As a result, reps reverted to old habits, and the business struggled to connect enablement efforts with performance outcomes.

In a modern world, we have the opportunity and the need for a fundamentally different model, one that addresses the limits of traditional enablement and meets the demands of modern selling. With AI, this model is not just theory. An enablement engine that is always on with an intelligent layer that reviews rep activity, curates personalized content, and delivers real-time feedback is now increasingly possible. This model drives enablement, replacing episodic training with continuous development embedded directly into the rep's workflow.

Surrounding this core are four interlocking pillars that fuel, activate, and optimize enablement across the field:

1. **Content—The foundation of field activation**
2. **Programs—Structured learning that scales**
3. **Sales Engagement Tools—Enablement in the flow of work**
4. **Analytics—The insight engine for improvement**

This flywheel represents the next evolution of enablement, one powered by AI and sustained by the operational systems and human accountability that bring it to life. Even with the most intelligent feedback loops, automation, and personalized delivery, it is the consistency of coaching, deal inspection, and manager engagement that ultimately drives behavior change. AI can power the system, but enablement still depends on people to make it real.

3.1 Content: The Foundation of Field Activation

Content is where enablement begins—and it's the first pillar of the flywheel for a reason. Before a rep can execute, coach, or optimize, they must first understand what good looks like, and that understanding starts with content. Content is the mechanism by which strategy becomes execution, turning abstract GTM goals into field-ready guidance. Content lays the foundation for every other pillar in the enablement flywheel, powering programs, enhancing tools, and surfacing insights through analytics.

If enablement is a system, then content is the source code—the language, structure, and logic that fuel every downstream motion. Without strong content, no program can scale, no coaching can stick, and no AI system can deliver the right prompt at the right time.

Effective enablement content moves reps from uncertainty to clarity. It simplifies the complex, aligns with what the business is trying to drive, and equips reps to act with confidence. When done right, content becomes the operating system for sales conversations, guiding reps through plays, helping them position value, and preparing them for the moments that matter most.

But content alone isn't enough. It must be built to scale, designed for delivery, and reinforced in motion. The following section outlines what great enablement content looks like—and what happens when we get it wrong.

What Good Content Looks Like: Modular by Design

Modular content is the foundation of scalable, flexible enablement. Each unit should be designed as a self-contained, easily consumable piece that can stand alone or snap into a broader sequence when needed. The goal is clarity, adaptability, and relevance in every format and context.

In practice, this means designing enablement content that:

- Focuses on a single clearly defined concept;
- Can be consumed in two to three minutes or less (think: Slack snippet, one-pager, or micro-video); and
- Is structured so it can be reused across channels, whether in onboarding, a live session, a call library, or a tool like Highspot or Notion.

Modular design supports:

- Personalization by role, segment, or seniority;
- Easier updates so you don't need to redo entire playbooks to reflect one change; and
- Embedding into rep workflows at the right moment without overwhelming them with information.

A common trap is long-form legacy content— twenty-slide decks, hour-long LMS videos, or bloated learning paths. These formats may feel comprehensive but are often overwhelming, repetitive, and quickly outdated. Worse, they're difficult to test against. If you can't create a focused knowledge check or role-play prompt, it's a sign the content is too broad to retain.

A practical test:

> *Could a rep absorb this, apply it, and be coached on it without needing to rewatch or reread the entire thing?*

When content is modular, enablement becomes lighter, faster, and more aligned with the pace of change in today's AI native organizations.

⦚ Field Note: The Power of Modularization in Onboarding

One of our early challenges in revamping onboarding was low prework completion. Many AEs were showing up to bootcamp without having completed their assigned modules, making it difficult for them to absorb content and harder for facilitators to hold them accountable.

When we investigated, the root cause became clear: The onboarding content in our LMS had ballooned to over sixty hours. Videos had been stacked onto learning paths over time, many of them repetitive and unstructured. Worse, it was hard to tell what the curriculum actually *was*. It was buried inside the LMS logic.

We audited every module, removed duplications, and restructured the content into discrete modular units, each focused on a single concept, ran two to three minutes long, and was paired with meaningful knowledge checks. We cut the content first to fifteen hours and eventually down to six without losing any core messaging.

The impact? One hundred percent of new hires completed their prework within two weeks. And for the first time, we had clarity on what reps were supposed to know, what they had actually completed, and where accountability belonged.

🔍 Key Watchouts:

- Don't confuse "breaking things up" with making them modular. Modularity means each unit has a clear objective and can stand alone or snap into a sequence.
- Avoid content that's too vague or broad to test. If you can't create a simple knowledge check, it's likely too abstract to be retained.
- Refrain from stacking videos or slides without structure: stacking ≠ sequencing
- Don't assume content will be reused just because it's short. Contextual tagging and labeling are what make modular content discoverable.

What Good Content Looks Like: Structured Around Shared Frameworks

Structured content is more than well-organized—it's built around a consistent framework that gives reps a repeatable way to think, speak, and sell. Whether it's the 3 Whys, Command of the Message, or your own value selling model, frameworks act as mental scaffolding that enables reps to internalize key concepts faster and apply them more effectively in real conversations.

A strong framework:

- Reduces cognitive load in the field;
- Speeds up onboarding and comprehension;
- Aligns how reps approach discovery, objection handling, and value delivery; and
- Creates a shared language across sales, marketing, and product.

Without structure, reps are left to decode content on their own, wasting valuable time and energy trying to extract meaning or repackage messaging for customer conversations. Worse, they begin to improvise inconsistently, which fragments the narrative and erodes credibility in the field.

But structure doesn't just matter inside sales. It must extend across the entire go-to-market organization.

✏️ Field Note: The Cost of Misaligned Messaging

At a previous company, we invested millions of dollars in training our sales team on a structured sales framework. Every part of the sales conversation was defined with precision—problem articulation, quantified impact, future state, required capabilities, and solution mapping.

But one thing was missing: Marketing was never brought into the framework.

As a result, the product marketing team continued producing customer-facing content in their own format, with a narrative flow completely disconnected from what reps had been trained to deliver. When reps received this raw content, it felt foreign and unusable. They couldn't quickly translate it into the familiar structure they'd internalized through training.

Enablement and sales teams ended up spending hours restructuring decks and rewriting positioning docs just to make the content consumable. Later, a significant portion of time was spent educating marketing on the need for shared structure and building bridges between content creators and the sales execution motion.

The takeaway? Sales frameworks should not live in sales alone. For structured content to be truly effective, it must be adopted and applied across the full GTM ecosystem—marketing, product, customer success—not just the sales floor.

🔍 Key Watchouts:

- Avoid introducing too many competing frameworks, which leads to confusion and inconsistency.
- Ensure your framework is used not just in onboarding decks but across all sales plays, campaigns, and customer-facing materials.
- Ask: *Can the sales team, marketing, and product leaders all explain our core message the same way?*

When structure is shared, sales execution becomes smoother, faster, and more consistent. When it's siloed, it becomes an internal translation problem that slows everything down.

What Good Content Looks Like: Aligned to GTM Priorities

Aligned content connects enablement efforts directly to what the business is driving—product launches, pricing shifts, competitive plays, or strategic campaigns. It helps reps understand the bigger picture: why this content matters now, how it ties into company goals, and what action is expected of them.

When content is aligned, it stops feeling like just another update; it becomes fuel for execution. Reps know not just what to say but why they're saying it and how that message reinforces broader market positioning.

One way to reinforce alignment is to embed current business priorities directly into training content. For example, when rolling out champion-building content during a major product launch, real product use cases and customer scenarios were embedded into the champion training. This allowed reps to immediately practice their skills in a relevant high-priority context, accelerating both content adoption and business impact.

But alignment isn't just about timing; it's about *intentional sequencing.* Too often, organizations release content as soon as it's ready without considering whether it's relevant, well timed, or coordinated with other initiatives. When this happens, reps experience it as noise. They feel overwhelmed, not enabled. Cognitive overload sets in. Confusion outweighs clarity.

At one company, the enablement team began positioning themselves as the "guardians of the content galaxy." The role wasn't to block content but to scrutinize it before it reached the sales floor, ensuring it was relevant, paced well, and integrated into the broader narrative. That sometimes meant saying "not now" to a product update or feature release. This wasn't because the content was wrong but because the timing, format, or delivery plan wasn't set up for rep success.

In many cases, the team didn't discard the content. Instead, they curated it. They reformatted, indexed, and organized it into the content library so reps could find it when it mattered most. Strategic enablement means delivering the right message at the right time in the right format, not delivering all messages at once.

🧪 Field Note: Show the Outcome, Not the Process

When we rolled out a new asset for the field—whether it was a calculator, talk track, or messaging one-pager —we focused not on teaching the asset but on demonstrating the outcome.

One of the most impactful examples was our business case calculator. It was powerful but fairly complex on the back end. The real value, however, was in the output: a polished, one-slide executive summary that reps could use directly in boardroom conversations.

Instead of running a training on how to use the calculator step by step, we brought in a few AEs who had already used it successfully. In our weekly enablement call, they walked the team through how they had used the calculator in a live deal and presented the actual customer-facing asset it produced.

That flipped the switch. Reps immediately saw the *why* behind the tool and understood the impact it could make in their deals. Adoption followed naturally. Once reps were sold on the outcome, they were eager to read the instructions. We didn't have to enforce usage—we simply had to sequence it around what mattered.

📕 *What We Mean by "Business Case Calculator"*

A business case calculator is a tool used to quantify the financial impact of a solution. It typically outputs a customer-facing summary, such as ROI, cost savings, or efficiency gains, in a format that supports executive conversations. These tools help buyers justify the investment internally by clearly articulating the business rationale for the purchase. While the back end may be complex, the value lies in the clarity and credibility of the outcome it helps reps deliver.

🔍 Key Watchouts:

- Don't push content just because it's ready. Align it with what the field is doing now.
- Beware of content competing for rep attention; every piece should earn its place in the rollout.
- Ensure product, marketing, and enablement roadmaps are synchronized so reps hear a single coherent message.

- Build temporal findability. Make sure content shows up *when* it's relevant, not just *where* it lives.

What Good Content Looks Like: Designed for Delivery Mode

Content must be structured with the delivery experience in mind. Even the most well-crafted message can fail to land if it's delivered in the wrong format, at the wrong time, or through the wrong channel. Design choices should be shaped not just by the content itself but by how and where it will be consumed—whether that's in a live ILT, a Slack thread, a self-paced LMS module, or a real-time copilot suggestion embedded in a tool.

A slide meant for a workshop needs different pacing, visual flow, and context than a one-pager intended for asynchronous review. A Slack drop of a talk track needs to be short, skimmable, and linked to relevance. And a live ILT session should not be used to teach dense material from scratch; rather it should be used to reinforce, practice, and land key concepts that have already been introduced.

Too often, organizations create content in one format and attempt to repurpose it across all others without redesign. For example, a live session recording is posted into an LMS as a course, or a slide deck used for training is handed to reps as is for customer use. But content built for interaction and facilitation often fails when flattened into passive formats. Rep engagement suffers, and the message loses impact.

To meet diverse learning styles and increase accessibility, each key concept should ideally be delivered in three to four complementary formats:

- A short video or animation
- A written summary or one-pager
- A live discussion or role-play
- A knowledge check or scenario-based quiz

This multiformat approach ensures the message is reinforced from different angles, and reps can engage with it in the way that works best for them—on their own time or in structured settings.

🧪 Field Note: Designing for Role-Play, Not Lecture

In one of our most effective ILT programs, we used a simple but powerful structure:

1. **Prereading or light prep homework (e.g., watch a video or review a real customer situation)**
2. **Ten to fifteen minutes of live instruction to set the context**
3. **Small-group breakout for hands-on scenario work (fifteen to twenty minutes)**
4. **Regroup and debrief, sharing real insights from the field**

But most importantly, we never used ILT to introduce new material. We used ILT to land it. One of my favorite sessions was on champion-building. In pairs, AEs had to coach each other in delivering the 3 Whys of their own deal while role-playing the champion they needed to activate. The goal wasn't just to recite messaging; it was to practice coaching someone external on how to tell the story back to the buyer team.

Because our enablement team owned both content design and facilitation, we had creative freedom to shape each session for how it would land in the field. For teams without that flexibility, the same principles apply: Don't start with slides—start with the rep's reality. Design backward from what they need to do in a live conversation, and structure the session to get them one step closer.

🔍 Key Watchouts:

- Avoid reusing content across delivery formats without rethinking structure, flow, and interactivity.
- Don't over-index on one format. Learners vary widely in how they absorb and apply information.
- ILTs are for activation, not information transfer. Save teaching for prework, and use live time for practice.
- Build in exercises that reflect actual sales conversations, not just theoretical knowledge.

When content is built with structure, validated by the field, and delivered in modular, context-aware formats, it stops being a static resource and becomes a catalyst for clarity and execution. It builds confidence, shortens ramp time, and equips reps to show up prepared in the moments that matter most. But on its own, even the best content isn't enough.

What transforms content into impact is what surrounds it—the programs that deliver it, the coaching that reinforces it, and the cadence that makes it stick. Content lights the path, but programs are what carry reps down it through repetition, application, and real-time adaptation. That's why enablement must go beyond assets and toolkits. It must be designed as a system of delivery that embeds learning into motion.

In the next section, we'll explore how to build enablement programs that do exactly that: drive action, scale consistently, and evolve with the needs of both the field and the business.

3.2 Programs: Structured Learning That Scales

If content is the foundation of enablement, then programs are the operating system that delivers that content with structure, repetition, and purpose. Programs are what turn insight into behavior. They sequence learning in a way that reflects both what the business needs now and what reps are ready to absorb. They're the connective tissue that translates strategic priorities into field execution.

Great programs don't attempt to teach everything at once. Instead, they focus on what matters most in the moment: the actions a rep needs to take this week, this quarter, or in the next conversation. This isn't just instructional design; it's enablement process design. For example, instead of beginning onboarding with a detailed walkthrough of personas, pricing models, or the entire sales process, we might begin with how to craft a compelling outbound message that ties directly to a known pain point. That's what gets a rep generating pipeline in week one—and that early momentum is far more valuable than theoretical readiness.

It's tempting to equate enablement programs with content delivery, but they're much more than content playlists. Programs are deliberate, time-bound learning systems that drive adoption, shift behaviors, and build durable habits across the team. Where content is modular by design, programs are about orchestration, delivering the right messages in the right sequence that are reinforced at the right depth and cadence.

Effective programs are not just well-structured—they are well-paced. They account for rep readiness, adapt to performance signals, and build progressively toward mastery. The best programs integrate peer collaboration, manager coaching, real-time inspection, and workflow-based reinforcement into a cohesive learning arc. A single enablement program might span days or weeks or unfold over a full quarter with pre-work, live sessions, team huddles, follow-ups, and inspection moments layered together to ensure sustained application.

Programs also act as the glue that binds the rest of the enablement flywheel together. They bring content to life, embed learning into tools, and generate the behavioral signals that analytics can use to surface insight. When done well, they create a closed loop where reps are guided forward, managers know how to coach, and enablement can adapt quickly to what's working in the field.

While specific program design will vary based on maturity, team structure, and GTM motion, several foundational types consistently drive results across high-performing sales organizations.

What follows is a breakdown of these core program types, which are structured by purpose, design philosophy, and real-world execution.

Onboarding: Designing the Full Learning Journey

The best onboarding programs do more than check a box. They build momentum. New hires arrive excited, curious, and ready to contribute. Great onboarding doesn't waste that energy. It channels it into meaningful action, building confidence and establishing early behaviors that lead to long-term success.

Too often, companies equate onboarding with a single event—a checklist to run through, a few linear

LMS video paths, or a one-week bootcamp. But onboarding is not a one-off training or isolated experience. It's a full journey designed to build habits, accelerate understanding, and support real-world application across time. A true onboarding program is an intentional learning journey that's structured to unfold across time, channels, and modalities. It weaves together prework, peer interaction, field assignments, live reinforcement, manager coaching, and milestone assessments into a single coherent arc.

That arc must be sequenced with care. The goal isn't to dump information. It's to activate learning, reinforce it through practice, and embed it through repetition. Strong programs start with foundational prework, lightweight materials that orient reps to language, concepts, and workflows. This early exposure ensures that reps show up to live sessions ready to engage, not just to listen.

Sales bootcamp in the form of ILT can play a valuable role in onboarding, but it is not the program itself. ILT is a delivery format, not a strategy. It should be used as a catalyst to deepen application, facilitate group learning, and accelerate confidence through role-play and discussion. But without upstream preparation or downstream follow-through, even the best ILT sessions lose their stickiness.

📓 What We Mean by "Sales Bootcamp"

Sales bootcamp typically refers to an intensive instructor-led experience delivered early in a rep's onboarding, often over several days. It's designed to accelerate familiarity with messaging, systems, and selling motion.

But a bootcamp is not a full onboarding program. It is one moment in the journey. Many organizations mistakenly treat bootcamp as the finish line, assuming that after a few days of immersion, reps are ready to execute. In reality, true onboarding requires consistent reinforcement, real-world application, and a longer runway to build durable behaviors. Bootcamp may build energy, but without a full program behind it, that energy fades fast.

✒ Field Note: Turning Virtual Onboarding into a System

During the COVID-19 shift to remote work, we faced this challenge head-on. Previously, onboarding was delivered through two 4-day in-person bootcamps (Sales I and Sales II), spaced three to four months apart. When we had to transition to virtual, replicating those intensive workshops over Zoom felt impossible— too long, too flat, too easy to disengage.

But the challenge pushed us to rethink the program. We redesigned onboarding into a twelve- to fifteen-week journey, delivered through ninety-minute sessions three to four times a week and paired with guided fieldwork in between. Instead of compressing all learning into four days, we sequenced it gradually, building context, layering skills, and aligning sessions with what reps were actually doing in the field.

What changed was not just the format but the philosophy. Reps didn't just attend onboarding—they were *in onboarding* over time. They brought live deal scenarios into group discussions. They practiced messaging with real objections. They applied each new concept and came back with questions, feedback, and peer insights.

The results were clear: Ramp productivity held steady, engagement improved, and the quality of conversation went up. Onboarding stopped being an event and became a system.

As hybrid work has been returning, I've been recommending a model that blends virtual learning for scale with in-person milestone days focused on cohort connection, peer presentations, and skill showcases. While I haven't yet seen this approach fully executed at a best-in-class level, I believe it represents the future of onboarding, one that honors both the flexibility of modern work and the enduring power of shared experiences.

🔍 Key Watchouts:

- Don't confuse sales bootcamp with onboarding. ILT is a format, not a program.
- Avoid launching a single bootcamp without upstream preparation or downstream reinforcement.

- Sequence learning over time. Think in arcs, not events.
- Build in opportunities for real-world application between sessions.
- Anchor the experience in community, accountability, and manager support, not just content delivery.

Ongoing Enablement: Turning Learning into a Ritual

Ongoing enablement is where learning becomes part of the rhythm of selling. It's not a one-time initiative but a continuous investment that reinforces skill development, message clarity, and deal execution.

We consistently found a strong correlation between reps who participated in ongoing enablement and those who outperformed on the job. This pattern reinforced a key insight: Enablement must be embedded into the weekly cadence. It should happen at the same time each week, be clearly expected by the team, and be prioritized by leadership rather than being treated as optional. That doesn't mean every rep will engage equally. But when the system is consistent, reps know where to find it, when to expect it, and how to lean in when the content matches their current needs. Over time, this rhythm builds stronger habits and better outcomes. Enablement stops feeling like an interruption and starts working like a lightweight, high-impact ritual. The most successful ongoing programs prioritize credibility and relevance. The messenger matters. Sessions led by marketing or product often feel top-down and instructional. But when programs are delivered by respected peers or field leaders—people who've been in the same customer conversations—they feel real. They feel earned. Reps listen more closely and apply what they hear.

Sales leaders that made development part of their ongoing cadence, whether it was in their team calls once a month or part of their quarterly business review (QBR) agendas, had a higher productivity and engagement rate. These are the same AEs that would continuously prioritize the mandatory calls and be the ones to complete their certifications first.

📖 What We Mean by "Quarterly Business Review (QBR)"

*A QBR is a structured quarterly forum where sales leaders bring their teams together to reflect on performance, inspect deals, and refocus for the upcoming quarter. The best QBRs are more than forecast reviews. They are moments for **inspiration, coaching, and accountability**. QBRs are a good moment to spotlight what's working, create space for rep reflection, and reinforce team-wide development.*

📖 Sample QBR Agenda

1. Team Performance Review
Celebrate highlights, attainment, and key wins from the previous quarter. Use this to set tone and energy.

2. Individual Rep Reviews
Each AE shares brief reflections, and public commitment builds accountability and trust across the team:

- *Their achievements (for the previous quarter)*
- *Their learnings (what worked and what didn't)*
- *Their forecast for the quarter*

3. Team Development Segment
Skill spotlight, sales play reinforcement, or breakdown of recent wins/losses. Designed to raise the team's executional fluency through shared learning.

4. Recognition and Prizes
Close with awards tied to both performance and behavior—celebrating consistency, creativity, growth, and execution.

✒ Field Note: Peer-Led Enablement That Stuck

At a previous organization, we ran a thirty-minute weekly enablement call. It was mandatory, but it didn't feel like a requirement. Reps showed up because every session featured a peer—an AE or SE—sharing a story, breaking down what worked, and offering practical takeaways. That peer-driven format created inspiration and accountability. Reps left with insights they could apply immediately, and they often stayed after to ask questions or go deeper.

The program became so successful that AEs were often clamoring to be featured. They took real pride in preparing for it, knowing this was their opportunity to lead from the front and earn peer recognition.

The lesson: Ongoing enablement works best when it's short, consistent, and community led. It shouldn't be an overload of new information. It should feel like a rhythm. A chance to reconnect to best practices, reinforce winning behaviors, and improve through shared learning. In the best cases, it doesn't just feel helpful. It feels cultural, a reminder that learning isn't an interruption to the job. It *is* the job.

Key Watchouts:

- Don't treat ongoing enablement as optional. It must be visible, expected, and backed by leadership to drive participation and results.

- Avoid overloading with new information. Use sessions to reinforce, not overwhelm. Focus on behavior, not breadth.
- Watch for top-down delivery fatigue. Peer-led or manager-facilitated sessions build more trust, credibility, and stickiness than HQ-led monologues.
- Don't neglect follow-through. Enablement should tie back to real metrics, in-the-field behaviors, or deal movement, not exist in a vacuum.
- Consistency beats novelty. Flashy one-offs fade fast; rituals that are repeatable and respected build a learning culture.

Leadership Enablement: Turning Managers into Multipliers

If enablement fuels the system, then frontline leaders are the levers. Leadership enablement is about equipping managers to be more than operators of performance—they must become developers of people. And like reps, leaders need structured support to grow, especially as their role in an AI native world evolves.

At its core, leadership enablement centers around helping managers master three foundational responsibilities:

Recruitment—Attracting and selecting talent that aligns with the team's values, motion, and culture. Managers need a clear definition of what great looks like and support in identifying, assessing, and onboarding against that standard.

Retention—Creating an environment where top talent stays and thrives. This includes building clarity around expectations, recognizing success, and enabling personal growth.

Revenue—Driving performance through targeted coaching and consistent reinforcement of key sales behaviors.

While these responsibilities are not new, how we support them must evolve. In an AI native world, enablement plays a critical role in helping leaders think differently about how to lead. Below are illustrative examples of what this can look like.

Recruitment

- Using AI to surface high-potential candidates based on attributes of top performers
- Offering structured interview guides aligned to success criteria
- Automating outreach and follow-up through copilot tools

Retention

- Nudging leaders to acknowledge rep milestones or intervene based on behavioral patterns
- Using performance signals to detect disengagement or burnout early
- Recommending enablement content tailored to an individual's gaps or goals

Revenue

- Providing deal and call insights before one-on-ones to focus conversations
- Flagging missed behaviors and suggesting coaching plays
- Automating next steps like follow-up notes or skill reinforcements based on recent activity

These are just examples. The broader point is that managers need support doing their real job, which is different from being a super rep. And with the right AI systems and coaching tools, managers can amplify enablement far beyond what a single program can deliver, and they do this work with greater precision and less manual lift.

Enablement's role is not just to provide resources but to instill a mindset of leadership development. This also means ensuring leaders are never caught off guard by what's being delivered to the field. Managers should have early access to any content, programs, or playbooks before rollout so they can internalize the material, ask questions, and prepare to coach effectively. Their understanding and buy-in are essential for consistency as well as credibility. When reps see their managers reinforcing enablement, not learning it alongside them, trust grows. And when managers are equipped early, they shift from passive observers to active multipliers.

When managers commit to their own cadence of growth and reflection, their teams follow suit. They set the tone—not just through words but by example.

Tactically, leadership enablement might include the following:

- Early always-on access to content so managers can coach it in real time per AE needs
- Training on how to interpret deal intelligence and metrics to uncover meaning, ask better questions, and spark coaching conversations, all augmented by conversational AI that helps leaders probe more deeply and identify key gaps

- Templates for effective 1:1s, pipeline reviews, and coaching conversations that can be assessed and acted on proactively, rather than relying solely on delayed or retrospective reviews
- Peer forums that facilitate the sharing of best practices and experiential learning, curated and surfaced at moments of need to address emerging challenges or patterns across the team

In a world of always-on enablement, leaders are the link between programs and performance. They ensure that skills are reinforced, not just introduced. And with the help of AI and enablement, they can focus on what matters most: building teams that grow, win, and stay.

📖 *What We Mean by "1:1s"*

1:1s are regular dedicated meetings between a manager and a rep. In a high-performing sales culture, they are not just status updates—they are coaching moments. Effective 1:1s focus on deal inspection, skill development, behavior reinforcement, and forward planning.

The most effective 1:1s follow a consistent agenda that sets shared expectations. Without structure, these meetings can drift, becoming therapy sessions for the rep or solely forecast reviews for the manager. A shared rhythm helps both parties stay aligned on what matters most: performance, development, and execution in the field.

In the enablement system, 1:1s are where learning is reinforced and rep behaviors are shaped over time.

📖 Effective 1:1 Agenda for AE Development

1. Development Plan and Metrics Review (ten to fifteen min.)

Review the rep's current development focus and inspect relevant leading indicators.

- *Are they doing what they committed to?*
- *Are behaviors aligned to the plan (e.g., number of meetings, outreach consistency, sales play execution)?*
- *Are there signs of progress or regression?*

2. Opportunity Review and Skill Gap Identification (fifteen to twenty min.)

Review key deals and use them to surface patterns in rep behavior.

- *Are discovery calls landing?*
- *Are deals getting stuck at a consistent stage?*
- *What skills are showing up or missing?*
- *Use this as a foundation for additional development goals.*

3. Rep Asks / Manager Support (five to ten min.)

Give the rep structured time to raise blockers, ask for help, or request feedback.

- *What's working?*
- *Where are they stuck?*
- *What support do they need from you or the broader organization?*

✒ Field Note: Building Confidence Through Leader-Only Development Calls

At each organization, we prioritized running dedicated leaders-only development calls focused on core management fundamentals. These sessions were designed to level-set expectations and equip sales managers—many of whom were first-time leaders—with the skills to inspire, coach, and inspect effectively.

Too often, high-performing reps are promoted into management without support under the false assumption that success will translate automatically. These calls gave new managers a safe space to ask questions, clarify leadership concepts, and align on what good looked like.

Over time, these sessions increased managerial confidence; they also helped set the tone for how leaders could model enablement behavior for their teams. Many of those same leaders went on to facilitate enablement sessions themselves, bringing added credibility and continuity to the learning culture.

The best sales organizations prioritize leadership development deliberately, carving out time during

SKOs or hosting dedicated offsites to invest in building sales leadership muscle. It's not a luxury—it's a requirement for sustainable performance.

🔍 Key Watchouts:

- Don't confuse high individual performance with leadership readiness. The best sellers don't always make the best managers. Without coaching and development, they default to being super reps.
- Avoid generic training. Leadership enablement must be contextualized to sales leadership, not broad corporate management principles.
- Beware of inspection without coaching. Metrics only matter if managers know how to act on them.
- Don't assume adoption without modeling. If leaders don't model the behaviors they're asking of reps, the system breaks down.

- Consistency matters. One leadership session won't change behavior. Build habits through regular reinforcement and reflection.

As we move from the structured delivery of enablement programs to the fluid reality of day-to-day selling, the next layer of the flywheel comes into focus: the tools that embed enablement into the rep's workflow.

Programs build habits through structure and repetition. But execution happens in motion—during research, on the call, while writing follow-ups, or reviewing pipeline. That's where sales engagement tools step in. These tools ensure that insights, content, and guidance don't just arrive once. They show up in context, when and where reps need them most. The result: a system that doesn't just train reps but supports and adapts with them in real time.

3.3 Sales Engagement Tools in an AI Native World

If content is the source code and programs are the operating system, then sales engagement tools are the real-time interface, the layer where enablement meets execution. These tools are the bridge between preparation and action, guiding reps at the moment of need.

Sales engagement tools form a critical outer ring of the enablement flywheel. They are what bring enablement to life in the flow of selling—delivering content, insight, and feedback in real time, then feeding that motion back into the core AI engine for continuous improvement (a concept we'll return to in the next section). Where programs create structure and rhythm, tools create responsiveness. They meet reps during research, on the call, while writing follow-ups, or reviewing pipeline, offering just-in-time support that feels like part of the work, not an extra step on top of it.

Historically, enablement tools were siloed. They tackled a narrow slice of the sales motion—content distribution, call transcription, outbound sequencing—without addressing the end-to-end experience of the rep. Legacy tools were reactive, solving discrete problems after they occurred. Today's AI native engagement stack is proactive, delivering the right action at the right moment in the right format.

This section breaks down sales engagement tooling into five categories:

- Enrichment and Intent—Tools that identify, prioritize, and qualify potential buyers based on firmographic, technographic, and behavioral signals
- Engagement—Platforms that help reps reach out, follow up, and stay connected through orchestrated outbound motion across email, calls, and social
- Coaching—Tools that capture calls, analyze rep behavior, and surface insights to managers or reps themselves, driving continuous skill development
- Insight—Systems that help reps and managers understand pipeline health, deal progression, and buyer behavior, turning activity into intelligence

- Productivity—Workflow tools that stream-line motion, remove friction, and automate repetitive tasks so reps can focus on selling

Each category is evolving in how it supports reps, and AI is unlocking new value across the board.

Enrichment and Intent

Traditional enrichment has long been measured by volume: how much data you could afford to purchase or license across various sources. This often relied on waterfall methods, sequentially pulling from multiple vendors until a record was filled. While this maximized completeness, it didn't guarantee accuracy or contextual relevance. Worse, it meant teams paid to enrich accounts they weren't even actively pursuing.

In contrast, AI native enrichment has the potential to flip the model. It focuses on accuracy, selectivity, and real-time contextualization. Rather than bulk-enriching a static list, AI systems prioritize enrichment based on what matters now: who a rep is prospecting, what territory is being worked, and which accounts show meaningful signals.

Some vendors are applying AI to parts of the enrichment process, advancing the category in meaningful ways, even if they don't yet reflect a fully AI native approach:

- **ZoomInfo** pioneered scalable enrichment by building robust datasets and layering predictive intent and scoring on top by integrating AI capabilities into their enrichment engine. It's a powerful foundation built for breadth, but it still leans on completeness and broad coverage as its core design principle.
- **Clay** has taken significant strides in automating prospect research through multi-source querying, customizable workflows, and trigger-based enrichment by embedding AI into how those signals are interpreted and applied. While Clay offers significant flexibility, it still operates largely on a waterfall model, pulling from data

sources sequentially to complete a record, often without sensitivity to deal motion or rep-level focus.

Both platforms represent important evolution from legacy enrichment models. But they remain largely data-first rather than workflow-first. This leaves room for more real-time, signal-driven orchestration.

The Case for AI Native Enrichment

This would make enrichment:

- Real-time: Surfaced the moment it's needed, not preloaded in bulk;
- Signal-driven: Based on prospecting activity or dynamic engagement cues; and
- Cost-efficient: Only enriching what's actionable, reducing wasted spend.

This approach doesn't just save money; it protects focus. Not all enrichment is useful across all accounts. When enrichment is applied indiscriminately, reps and sales ops end up buried in irrelevant data. For example, enriching an entire book of accounts might surface details about subsidiaries or contact hierarchies that a rep will never use, cluttering CRM views and making it harder to act on real signals.

One emerging outcome of AI native enrichment is its impact on territory planning. Rather than revisiting account assignments quarter over quarter, enrichment data can be dynamically surfaced based on live signals, helping reps focus only on what's relevant in the moment. This shift makes territory planning continuous, not episodic, and reduces noise by eliminating the need to enrich or prioritize accounts that aren't in play.

📓 What We Mean by "Territory Planning"

Territory planning is the process of assigning sales reps to accounts or regions to ensure balanced coverage, reduce conflict, and maximize opportunity. Traditionally, this happens on a fixed quarterly or annual schedule.

📖 *What We Mean by "Book of Accounts"*

A book of accounts refers to the set of customers or prospects assigned to a rep. It defines where the rep is expected to engage, generate pipeline, and drive revenue.

AI native enrichment moves us away from "just in case" data acquisition toward a "just in time" model that's leaner, smarter, and directly tied to revenue motion.

AI native enrichment is:

- Always-on: Continuous sync across sources, not just a waterfall lookup;
- Change aware: Triggered by meaningful shifts (new buyer activity, intent spikes, segment movement); and
- Personalized: Tailored to the rep's territory, pipeline, product focus, and personal strengths.

This removes guesswork, helping reps engage the right accounts at the right time with insight that feels fresh, not stale.

Engagement

Engagement refers to how sellers connect with customers at scale across multiple channels such as email, phone, social, and beyond. Much of today's engagement tooling still relies on standardization, template-based messaging tied to generic ideal customer profiles (ICP) or personas, delivered through linear cadences. For example, a prospect might receive a generic five-step sequence with scheduled emails sent on day one, day three, and day seven, regardless of whether they've shown interest, visited the website, or engaged with prior outreach. This kind of fixed timing ignores both buying and personalized signals—such as curiosity, role-based interest, or social engagement—and often feels impersonal or out of sync with the buyer's actual journey.

Instead of waiting for an arbitrary three-day delay, a more effective approach might look for signals like a buyer revisiting the pricing page or clicking on a customer case study. Those cues tell us something is happening, and they should prompt outreach that feels timely, not robotic.

What's also changed is the buyer. Today's buyers are more sophisticated and also more guarded. They're not looking to be sold to in a traditional sense; they want to be engaged with, educated, and respected. Sellers must earn the right to a conversation by demonstrating insight and personal relevance, not just persistence or polished templates.

As a result, the purpose of engagement has evolved. It's no longer about pushing messages—it's about building bridges. Outreach should create connection, not pressure. The goal is to open a door based on mutual interest, not force one open through automated repetition.

Engagement has become a two-way street. Sellers must be able to read buyer cues and respond with relevance. It's a shift from outreach to dialogue, from outreach automation to relationship momentum.

In today's environment, where buyer titles shift and roles blur, generic sequencing misses the mark. Buyers expect messaging that reflects their individual context. They want to feel known, not categorized.

The next evolution of engagement should then be about scaling personalization, making each prospect feel like the message was crafted just for them, tied to their role, their account, or even their individual signals. This requires more than tailoring based on persona; it means dynamically adjusting outreach to reflect who the buyer is, what they've done, and when they're engaging.

In this model, sequencing also becomes signal-based—triggered by real-time activity like a LinkedIn connection, a website visit, or an email open—not arbitrary delays like "send day three follow-up." AI native engagement tools are adaptive and dynamic, evolving with the conversation and the context.

Some may wonder if this kind of dynamic engagement is really new or if it's simply a return to good selling fundamentals. In many ways, it is. Great sellers have always adapted to buyer signals and earned trust through relevance. But even the best sellers benefit from support. The challenge isn't skill—it's capacity. The sales cycle has too many threads to track and too many moments to get right. Now, there's technology that can help. AI isn't here to automate the relationship. It's here to clear the noise, surface what matters, and help sellers show up at their best: more prepared, more present, and more precise.

📕 *What We Mean by "Signals"*

Signals are observable buyer behaviors, like opening an email, visiting a pricing page, rewatching a demo, or engaging on LinkedIn. These are behaviors that indicate interest, intent, or opportunity. The right signals, surfaced at the right time, reduce guesswork and increase relevance across the sales motion.

AI enables:

- Adaptive sequencing: Outreach adjusts based on signals, sentiment, and success;
- Style matching: Messaging tailored to the seller's voice and the buyer's preferences; and
- Multichannel orchestration: Conversations connected across email, call, social, and chat.

These tools don't just enable outreach. They transform it from a one-way broadcast into a two-way exchange. Modern engagement is more of a conversation—or even a dance—where sellers and buyers respond to each other's signals in real time. It's about creating space for interaction, curiosity, and timing, not just delivering information.

What today's tools get right:

- **Salesloft** and **Klenty** are both traditional sales engagement platforms that have made notable strides by incorporating AI into their workflows. Salesloft has integrated generative AI to help sellers draft buyer communications faster and with more contextual nuance. Klenty has introduced auto-engagement based on buyer intent signals, supporting multichannel outreach that responds in real time. While neither is fully AI native, both show how existing platforms are adapting to evolving engagement needs.
- **Regie.ai** is a newer platform that was built with AI at its core. It combines persona-driven outreach generation with intent

signals and campaign orchestration, moving closer to a true AI native engagement model. While Regie.ai continues to expand its orchestration capabilities, it reflects the design philosophy that underpins where the category is heading. To fully meet the vision of AI native engagement outlined here, platforms like Regie.ai would need to extend orchestration beyond message generation, coordinating across channels, dynamically adjusting in real time based on buyer behavior, and integrating contextual data across tools and teams.

These advances represent progress, but they still operate in parts: generating a message or triggering a step. What's needed next is orchestration—where content, timing, channel, and buyer context all work together in one intelligent loop.

By surfacing a 360-degree view of prior engagement and current signals, AI native engagement tools empower reps to tailor their outreach with precision, engage meaningfully, and move deals forward with confidence.

Coaching and Insight

Traditional tools delivered insights. At the same time, coaching was traditionally deferred to post-call reviews and manager-led feedback loops. Managers might get dashboards or call summaries, but without guidance on how to act, coaching remained inconsistent, reactive, or skipped altogether. Worse, many reps saw coaching as inspection, not development.

In an AI native world, coaching and insight are no longer separate functions. They're fused and designed to surface actionable insight in the moment to help reps improve over time.

AI native coaching tools do three things well:

- Real-time prompts: During calls or deal reviews, AI flags missed cues or opportunities and suggests in-the-moment adjustments.

- Retrospective intelligence: Post-call analytics identify patterns (e.g., talk time, objection handling, next steps) and map them to outcomes.
- Manager assist: AI generates coaching plans based on rep trends, deal context, and behaviors, taking the guesswork out of where to focus.

Together, these tools create just-in-time coaching, delivered at scale with context. Reps get personalized feedback aligned to their style, their pipeline, and their learning pace. Managers can coach more consistently without needing to manually sift through hours of calls or reports.

Today, most coaching still happens in static reviews or deal forecast sessions, often limited to calls and CRM data. Tools like **Gong** have made excellent strides in improving how conversational data is captured and analyzed, surfacing insights that help managers spot coaching moments across reps and conversations. But even Gong's* insights remain largely

---

* Gong analyzes sales conversations and provides post-call analytics, helping surface coaching opportunities based on patterns like

tethered to the post-call layer. The real opportunity is moving from retrospective coaching to proactive workflow-integrated support.

Other platforms like **SalesMagic** and **AdamX.ai** point to where this is heading. Their AI-driven role-play features let reps simulate conversations with synthetic personas modeled after real buyers, giving managers a chance to coach *before* a live call takes place. This begins to shift coaching from inspection to preparation, enabling higher quality execution in the moments that matter.

But coaching shouldn't be confined to those narrow windows. With AI orchestrating across the full sales workflow, coaching can now be embedded across all touchpoints—Slack threads, outbound engagement, product demos, and even internal collaboration moments. These signals all tell a story about rep effectiveness, and AI can use them to surface relevant, contextual coaching in moments that would have previously been overlooked.

---

talk ratios, objections, or missing next steps. However, its coaching remains focused on the call layer and does not offer full orchestration across sales workflows.

What's changing now is not just the presence of coaching but the timing and precision of it. Instead of reviewing a call after the fact, AI can now deliver guidance *during* the interaction—or even *before* it happens. For example, reps could simulate a real call by role-playing against an AI-trained persona of the actual buyer, pulling from past interactions, account context, and role-specific nuances. Managers can then step in to coach during that rehearsal, not days later.

With large language models (LLMs) trained specifically for sales methodology, coaching can also become more structured and strategic. These models can map conversations or behaviors to frameworks like MEDDPICC®* or Command of the Message, identifying areas for improvement in real time. They could even generate coaching plans proactively, cross-referencing deal performance, rep behaviors, product knowledge, and relationship signals to surface targeted recommendations for manager action.

---

* MEDDPICC® is a qualification framework and registered trademark of the MEDDIC Academy, developed by Dick Dunkel and Jack Napoli during their time at PTC. It is referenced here for context only.

This shift reframes coaching as an embedded feedback loop, not an afterthought. And when paired with personalized data—such as individual rep performance trends, deal engagement history, product proficiency, CRM behavior patterns, and even learning preferences—it becomes one of the highest-leverage tools in the entire enablement stack.

The future of coaching is contextual, dynamic, and AI-orchestrated, enabling both reps and managers to grow continuously, not episodically.

Productivity: From Task Automation to Strategic Orchestration

Productivity tools are often seen as tactical utilities. These tools shave off time, automate steps, or reduce clicks. In an AI native enablement system, their role must be more strategic. These tools should help sellers reclaim focus, increase consistency, and elevate performance, not just by saving time but by improving how time is used.

The issue with most of today's productivity tools is that they solve symptoms, not the root problem.

Many were built to address isolated friction points: speeding up CRM updates, simplifying outbound email writing, or automating recurring tasks. But productivity also includes how reps find and use information, from searching across systems to locating the right asset to aligning with internal teams.

These are all meaningful components of a rep's workflow, but they remain fragmented. Most tools accelerate a slice of the job without orchestrating the full motion. The result is faster execution but not necessarily better decisions.

Most are still confined to the system they were built for—CRM updates, email composition, task execution—and they rarely integrate meaningfully with surrounding sales context. They don't take into account what's happened across channels, within the account, or throughout the broader engagement. The result is workflow automation without orchestration. Reps still carry the cognitive burden of stitching information together, figuring out what matters, and deciding what to do next.

Some tools are beginning to address these gaps:

- **Clari** tackled CRM update fatigue by providing pipeline visibility and forecasting overlays, helping reps and managers stay aligned without manual entry. With the introduction of Clari Copilot, the platform has expanded to provide AI-generated call summaries, opportunity insights, and proactive nudges aimed at helping reps take next steps and prioritize more effectively across their pipeline.

- **Motion** is redefining sales productivity by using AI to manage time, tasks, and focus. It builds intelligent daily schedules that respond to shifting priorities, meeting loads, and deadlines, essentially acting as an AI-powered executive assistant for sellers. While not purpose-built for GTM workflows, it exemplifies how AI can help reps reduce context switching and spend more time on high-value activity. Its broader scope points to what AI native productivity orchestration could look like when integrated deeply into sales motion.

Much of today's tooling is still generative and reactive, confined to the immediate task or system it's built within. The next evolution is proactive and orchestrated, surfacing what to do next, why it matters, and how to act on it across the full selling motion.

AI native productivity tools should do three key things:

- Act as digital chiefs of staff: Nudging reps to follow up, reengage stalled deals, prep for meetings, or revisit a priority account
- Automate repetitive tasks: Drafting recap emails, logging CRM notes, updating fields, and suggesting logical next steps based on context

- Spark strategic thinking: Recommending relevant plays, outreach approaches, or enablement content based on deal stage, persona, or historical outcomes

Few tools deliver all three consistently today, but this framing offers a useful way to assess where AI is truly enabling rep performance versus just speeding up tasks.

These tools are not meant to replace rep judgment—they selectively absorb it. By taking over low-leverage, repetitive decisions, they preserve rep energy for the most critical thinking: building relationships, navigating complex buyer dynamics, and solving problems that require true insight.

For example, instead of deciding when to send a follow-up email or which asset to attach, a rep could be guided to focus on preparing for a high-stakes customer meeting, armed with AI-suggested talking points, competitive context, and a summary of past conversations. The tool takes care of the executional details so the rep can stay present, thoughtful, and strategic.

Too often, sellers report spending the majority of their time not meeting with customers but navigating internal systems, updating data, and managing task lists. Productivity tools should reverse this imbalance. Their goal should be to remove the barriers that prevent reps from doing the work that truly matters—whether that's preparing for strategic conversations, following up with insight, or collaborating with buyers across channels.

The power of AI native productivity tooling lies in its orchestration. When designed to work as part of the broader enablement loop—alongside coaching, content, and insight—these tools become multipliers. They reinforce best practices in the flow of work, reduce decision fatigue, and close the gap between intention and execution. Earlier examples, like pipeline-aware nudges tied to sales plays, meeting summaries that feed into manager coaching, or scheduling tools that prioritize rep learning time, show how even isolated tools can begin to embed into the broader enablement rhythm. The more deeply these tools connect with the actual motions of selling, the more leverage they create.

The outcome isn't just speed; it's precision, consistency, and quality at scale. These tools should ultimately shift the sales motion from reactive task execution to intentional customer engagement, enabling reps to spend more time in meaningful conversations with less time in operational drag. Whether it's removing the need to manually prioritize accounts or reducing the back-and-forth of internal coordination, AI native productivity tooling should elevate rep focus by absorbing complexity, not adding to it.

3.4 The AI Native Enablement Loop

The tools covered in the previous sections—enrichment, engagement, coaching, and productivity—each solve important pieces of the enablement puzzle. But even the best tools fall short when they operate in isolation. What's needed now is orchestration: a unified, AI native system that connects these elements into a continuous, adaptive loop.

At the center of this model is an intelligent orchestration layer, one that captures signals, analyzes behaviors, and delivers personalized guidance across every moment in the sales workflow. This isn't just about supporting reps more efficiently. It's about transforming enablement from a set of disconnected actions into a cohesive system that scales performance.

Where traditional enablement was episodic—content was launched, programs delivered, and feedback lagged—it was also fragmented. Content and programs were often delivered through disparate tools, making it difficult to connect the dots across rep behavior, deal context, and training touchpoints. The only question we could hope to answer was "Did this training land?"

The modern enablement engine is always on. It curates content, identifies gaps, reinforces behavior, and evolves continuously with the field. It's not an overlay; it's the operating system for enablement in the AI era. With this new model being real-time, embedded, and responsive, a more critical question is answered: "What does this rep need right now to move the deal forward?" And we get answers with precision, context, and speed.

AI makes this not just possible but imperative.

Core Principles of the AI Native Enablement Engine

To truly unlock performance at scale, this orchestration layer needs to operate by a new set of principles, each designed to drive velocity, precision, and consistency in the field. The system must be the following:

- Conversational—The system operates in natural language. Reps and managers engage with it like a teammate, asking questions, getting guidance, and clarifying next actions in the flow of work. This reduces friction and makes insight more accessible.
- Agentic—The system doesn't just inform; it takes meaningful action. Whether nudging a rep to reengage a stalled deal, drafting a personalized follow-up, or queuing targeted learning, it behaves like a proactive copilot that takes action on behalf of the rep. It accelerates motion and extends rep capacity.

- Real Time—Context decays quickly in sales. This system captures intent signals, content engagement, and behavioral data as it happens, delivering in-the-moment guidance when it's most relevant. This increases relevance, minimizes lag, and accelerates deal cycles.

- Self-Improving—With every interaction, the system learns, refining what content lands, what coaching works, and what behaviors lead to outcomes. Over time, it adapts to each rep's motion and raises the performance ceiling of the entire team, creating a smarter, more personalized enablement loop.

- Embedded—Intelligence must show up where reps work: inside CRM, email, Slack, and call platforms. No extra logins. No tool switching. It drives adoption, improves decision speed, and reduces context switching.

Here's how each pillar of the flywheel evolves in this model:

Content: Curated, Contextual, and Continuous

In the AI native loop, content doesn't just sit in a library. It moves. It's curated in real time based on deal context, rep behavior, and surfaced gaps. Today, most teams are just beginning to adopt AI in this space, primarily using prompt-based tools like **Jasper.ai** to generate content more efficiently. Platforms like **Highspot** and **Seismic** have also recognized this shift, layering AI to enhance content discoverability, tagging, and search. These enhancements reflect the broader market's recognition that delivering the right content at the right time is no longer a nice-to-have but a foundational requirement.

In contrast to static, role-based content models, the AI native system continuously learns what lands, what's ignored, and dynamically adjusts recommendations to maximize impact. This learning extends not only to what content works but who it works for, based on signals like asset views, click-throughs, call usage, deal outcomes, and rep feedback. If one rep consistently succeeds with a particular story, the system can automatically lean in, agentically adjusting decks to feature certain case studies, tailoring narrative framing to match their delivery style, and even suggesting alternate assets that align with their strengths. Content becomes not just personalized to the buyer but optimized for the rep.

To deliver value in this new model, content must move beyond access and availability to become timely, tailored, and actionable.

Aligned with the guiding principle of design for action, not just information transfer, content is delivered not simply because it exists, but because it is timely, relevant, and directly actionable by the rep. For example, a talk track surfaced right before a customer call or a case study triggered when pricing concerns arise.

Newer solutions like **Lavender.ai** and **Copy.ai** have been designed from the ground up with AI at their core, and they represent promising steps toward dynamic, adaptive content delivery. They are beginning to explore AI-generated messaging tailored to buyer context and sequencing logic. However, while they have strong foundations, current capabilities are still limited. For example, they often operate within the email workflow and do not yet adapt content delivery based on broader sales signals or behavior across systems. Their architecture may allow for broader orchestration in the future. Today, however, the system-wide coordination necessary for true enablement is still emerging.

Imagine a world where every piece of content reaches the rep at the moment of highest impact, content that is tailored not only to their customer and deal stage but also to how they learn, think, and deliver. Content is no longer one-size-fits-all. It's adaptive, data-driven, and tightly coupled to outcomes, transforming modular assets into a living, evolving system of enablement that meets the moment and individual every time.

Programs: Sequenced to the Moment of Need

Most enablement programs today are built for consistency, not context. Despite good intentions, they rely on standardized tracks—like 30-60-90-day onboarding or

LMS-based learning plans—that don't adapt to the rep's actual performance, behavior, or deal environment.

This leads to three core problems:

- Content and training often feel misaligned with the rep's immediate challenges.
- High performers are held back by linear tracks.
- Struggling reps are overwhelmed with irrelevant or mistimed material.

In an AI native model, programs are no longer scheduled by calendar but sequenced by context. Instead of relying on completion-based tracks, AI listens to behavioral signals—such as objections missed on calls, deals stalling, or lack of pipeline creation—and customizes programming in real time.

This shows up across all three major program types:

- Onboarding becomes milestone-based, not time-based, allowing high performers to accelerate and slower learners to receive targeted reinforcement.

- Ongoing development is cohorted dynamically based on shared patterns like objections, pipeline challenges, or skill gaps. Signals such as deal progression, missed coaching moments, content engagement, and learning activity shape training delivery.

- Leadership enablement becomes system assisted. Each rep receives a custom development path that is easy for the manager to monitor and support. AI synthesizes performance signals and suggests focus areas, removing the burden of manual plan creation.

AI not only personalizes but prioritizes, helping reps focus on what matters most right now.

The technical capability now exists to realize these AI native models, but most organizations haven't yet built the systems required to harness them in practice.

This is not about pushing more content. It's about reducing noise. Programs evolve with the rep, reinforcing confidence and precision instead of confusion and overload. Enablement becomes a responsive system of development, sequenced to the moment of need, not the page number in a curriculum.

The shift to AI native programming doesn't just accelerate development. It ensures that learning is relevant, timely, and tied to performance outcomes.

The Market Knows the Destination, But Not How to Get There

What's notable is that many vendors in the market are already aligned on the destination: enablement that is outcome linked, behaviorally triggered, and always relevant. But rather than pursuing orchestration through unified AI systems, most are trying to assemble it through composed mechanisms, connecting LMS platforms, call data, CRM signals, and analytics dashboards in fragile configurations.

For example:

- **Mindtickle + Gong** offers a promising pairing of signal and diagnostics, helping identify rep-level gaps based on real-time conversation data. However, it still relies on manual interpretation and lacks the ability to autonomously deliver programmatic interventions in the flow of work.

- **Saleshood** is leading on outcome-aware cohort programming, using AI to analyze learning data and predict likely performance. This reflects the market's recognition that behavior-driven, personalized enablement is the path forward. However, the platform still depends heavily on admin input to trigger and manage these programs rather than doing so agentically.

- **GTM Buddy** is another platform showing promise. It integrates learning delivery directly into the seller's workflow based on real-time triggers and deal context. Rather than requiring LMS logins or static paths,

GTM Buddy's approach brings learning into the rep's moment of need, aligned with motion, buyer behavior, and sales stage. While it still operates within a composed ecosystem, it points toward what AI native orchestration could look like when designed with workflow-first, behavior-driven principles.

Unlike content or engagement, most programming solutions have not yet made meaningful strides toward becoming AI native, though early signs of progress are beginning to emerge. This remains the largest opportunity in enablement, where the gap between ambition and execution is still widest.

The gap isn't in vision—it's in execution. Despite aligning on the need for personalized, outcome-driven enablement, most systems still fall short because they are not truly AI native. They lack the conversational interfaces that allow reps and managers to engage naturally and the agentic capabilities that push the right content or coaching at the right moment, without manual setup. The result is friction, delay, and inefficiency; enablement remains reactive, not responsive. Teams remain stuck stitching systems together. Reps and managers are left guessing and navigating complexity when they should be receiving clarity. Without true agentic orchestration, personalization remains incomplete and enablement remains expensive to scale. We'll explore why this gap persists and what it takes to close it in Section 4.

Sales Engagement Tools: Embedded, Adaptive, and Orchestrated

While sales engagement tools power specific motions—enrichment, outreach, coaching, and productivity—they've historically operated as isolated systems. Reps were left stitching together tasks across platforms, and managers were forced to interpret siloed dashboards to identify gaps. AI native orchestration changes this entirely.

These tools become context-aware, coordinated, and personalized. They don't just support task management. They proactively guide the rep. Insights, content, and actions are delivered not in bulk, but in sequence, shaped by buyer signals, deal movement, and rep behavior. The experience shifts from tool-driven work to flow-based selling.

What changes in the AI native model:

- Tools are embedded where reps already work—CRM, Slack, email, and call platforms—eliminating friction and increasing adoption.
- Sequences evolve dynamically based on live behavior—such as email engagement, objection triggers, or channel preference—replacing static calendars with responsive orchestration.
- Insights are surfaced in context, not dashboards; missed personas, pricing hesitations, or content gaps are paired with drafted follow-ups or targeted plays.
- Coaching becomes anticipatory, not reactive. Managers are prompted with intervention opportunities before the next 1:1, based on patterns, not postmortems.

- The system learns each rep's voice, style, and buyer dynamics and offers personalized support that aligns with how they work and communicate.

Rather than overwhelm, these tools relieve decision fatigue by narrowing focus, reinforcing what's working, and nudging reps toward targeted improvements.

AI native engagement tools don't just make sales faster. They make it smarter.

Platforms like **UnifyGTM** are beginning to embody this shift. Built from the ground up for orchestration, UnifyGTM listens across tools, interprets real-time seller and buyer signals, and prompts next actions directly in the flow of work. Whether it's surfacing a call summary, suggesting content based on persona and stage, or triggering a follow-up sequence based on account activity, UnifyGTM reduces noise while reinforcing consistency.

While still evolving, it reflects what the next generation of sales engagement systems will look like: connected, contextual, and agentic. And when orchestrated within the broader enablement loop, they turn every system into a signal, every insight into action, and every interaction into progress.

Analytics: Intelligence in Motion

Analytics no longer lives in isolated dashboards, where it is accessed after the fact and disconnected from action. In the AI native enablement loop, analytics is woven into the very fabric of how the system operates. Signals from content usage, call behavior, and CRM activity don't just inform analytics; they drive the loop. Each insight becomes part of a continuous feedback mechanism, powering real-time decisions and reinforcing every pillar of enablement with precision.

Reps see how they're tracking as they work. Managers are guided to high-impact coaching moments. Enablement knows what to adjust, even before lagging indicators show up. The loop doesn't just close; it sharpens with each turn.

Analytics in this model is both compass and accelerator. Every rep action—missed follow-up, standout message, underused asset—becomes fuel for optimization. But the true power isn't in measurement. It's in surfacing context-rich insights when and where they matter, and that's embedded inside workflows, not adjacent to them.

As reps engage, the system learns and delivering coaching, real-time nudges, and tailored corrections based on segment, role, and behavior. Analytics becomes the connective tissue between strategy and execution.

Consider this example: A customer raises a competitive objection over email, then expresses curiosity about a key capability on a discovery call with two different stakeholders. AI detects and connects those signals without any tagging required. Before the next meeting, the system surfaces a tailored insight: "This account is surfacing competitive concern and product curiosity. Here's the recommended talk track." Simultaneously, the manager receives a targeted coaching prompt that is contextualized to the deal and the rep's performance history. Insight becomes coordinated action and all in real time.

AI native vendors like **Revvolution.ai** and **TigerEye** are starting to reflect this vision. Revvolution.ai embeds real-time deal and rep-level analytics directly into sales workflows, surfacing timely coaching opportunities, forecasting insights, and behavior-driven nudges without the need for manual tagging or dashboards. TigerEye provides forward-looking analytics by tying rep behavior to pipeline movement and risk factors, enabling proactive intervention rather than reactive reporting. Both tools are designed with AI native foundations, aiming to turn insight into action in the moment.

While each platform exhibits strengths in embedding and contextual analytics, full AI native orchestration—where insights automatically trigger actions across systems—is still an area for growth.

Ultimately, analytics isn't just about tracking performance. It's about making intelligence the operating system of the go-to-market engine, fueling every interaction, shaping every motion, and closing every loop with clarity.

The Vision Is Within Reach

This future isn't a distant dream. It's already beginning to take shape. Conversational AI, in-flow nudges, and adaptive content delivery are no longer pilot experiments—they're active components of forward-thinking enablement stacks. These are not isolated innovations. They are the early scaffolding of a continuous, contextual, and outcome-driven system.

The ultimate promise of this model is that it improves with every use. Each coaching moment, deal interaction, and seller behavior feeds the loop, driving smarter guidance, faster adaptation, and more precise reinforcement.

But it's not just that the insights get better. As intelligence compounds, the system begins to act agentically, responding in real time and taking action *as a great rep would*. This frees sellers to focus on what only humans can do: building trust, navigating nuance, and solving problems in motion.

Over time, enablement shifts from reactive programming to a unified, intelligent engine for growth—one that works alongside the rep, not just behind them.

It's a stretch but not out of reach. The foundational elements are already here.

More importantly, the outcomes we've described—timely coaching, adaptive learning, precision engagement—

aren't just idealistic goals. They're what the market is already expecting. Organizations are actively investing in tooling, content, and workflows to enable this kind of behavior. The challenge isn't one of desire but of execution. Many are assembling the pieces but struggling to connect them into a cohesive system.

The next step is integration, orchestration, and execution at scale. That's what we'll explore in Section 4: what it will take to truly operationalize the AI native enablement loop.

4

What's Needed to Get There

While pieces of the AI native enablement loop are beginning to emerge—from Slack-based nudges to CRM-integrated copilots—most deployments remain fragmented and reactive. They mirror the form of the flywheel but lack the reasoning that powers it and are unable to interpret signals, adapt dynamically, or coordinate across the loop.

What's missing isn't effort—it's contextualization. Many teams are assembling the right parts; they've invested in point solutions, added AI to content generation, installed dashboards, and plugged in productivity tools. But these investments remain siloed. Signals don't trigger coordinated action. Insights don't flow into real-time execution.

Frontline behaviors remain disconnected from the systems that are supposed to support them.

Most enablement systems weren't designed to think. They were designed to deliver. Even current AI tools were built to generate, not to reason. That's why even with AI stitched in, the system still reacts instead of reasons. Tooling is passive. Programs are fixed. And while impact is visible in isolated moments, it isn't sustained or scalable.

AI can't simply be bolted onto legacy foundations. It must be embedded, woven into the workflows, data, and decisions that define execution. AI should replace stitched-together workflows with orchestration and fragmented data with shared context. It should connect insights to action in real time and learn from every interaction.

At the heart of this gap is data, more specifically the lack of unified, contextual access to the right data at the right time. Without it, AI systems can't reason, adapt, or guide the rep effectively in the moment.

This next section explores what that foundation requires—technically, operationally, and organizationally— and what it will take to deliver consistent, adaptive performance across every rep and motion.

📓 *What We Mean by "Designed to Think or Reason"*

A system that's "designed to think" does more than store information or execute rules. It can observe, interpret, and respond based on context. In an AI native enablement system, this means connecting multiple signals (like rep behavior, deal stage, or buyer engagement) and reasoning through what matters most in the moment.

__Reasoning__ is what allows a system to determine why something is happening, not just what is happening. For example, it's the difference between noticing a stalled deal and recommending a specific reengagement play based on what worked in similar scenarios.

These systems move from reaction to intentional orchestration, such as surfacing the right content, nudges, or coaching based on the full picture, not isolated inputs.

And in an AI native world, the goal isn't for the AI to think for us. It's to help us become better thinkers. The best systems don't just automate action; they elevate the rep's judgment, clarify reasoning, and guide human decisions with greater context and confidence.

4.1 Why the AI Native Loop Remains Out of Reach

Most enablement stacks were designed for static content delivery and one-time programs. Even the most modern systems are often stitched together with fragile integrations, asynchronous workflows, and fragmented intelligence.

These constraints create the following limitations, both technical and human:

- Content is static and disconnected from real-time rep activity.
- Programs are delivered in bulk rather than sequenced based on behavior or context.
- Tools are helpful but fragmented, adding friction instead of streamlining workflows.
- Analytics is retrospective, reliant on dashboards instead of driving live decisions.

Many of the behaviors described in the previous section—adaptive sequencing, proactive coaching, real-time analytics—are already technically possible.

But in practice, they are often implemented as composed workarounds on top of federated systems. For example, AI-generated summaries may be pulled from call recordings but are not synchronized with deal context or CRM data. Sales reps may receive content recommendations in Slack, but they're disconnected from deal stage, persona, or prior conversations. Managers may receive nudges in a dashboard but have no way to act on them directly in flow.

These disjointed efforts represent surface-level intelligence, which is informative but not effortlessly actionable. Each new tool increases complexity, not clarity, which has forced RevOps and Enablement to spend more time integrating systems than enabling reps. Tools exist in isolation. Intelligence may be generated, but it's not orchestrated.

Without a system that reasons across moments and connects insight to action, the flywheel cannot spin with consistency or scale.

4.2 Why These Limitations Exist

The limitations of today's architecture aren't accidental. They're a product of design decisions optimized for a different era. SaaS-based systems were built to deliver value through modular applications, integrations, and dashboards. But they weren't built to reason across context, act autonomously, or surface insights in real time.

In a world where context changes by the hour and the margin for error is razor thin, legacy architectures fall short. Built on fragile API bridges and asynchronous update cycles, these systems create gaps in insight, broken workflows, and delayed actions. This creates lags in insight, fractured workflows, and delayed actions. As a result, enablement teams scramble to keep up, and reps are left without clear direction in moments that matter most.

This isn't just a tooling problem—it's an execution gap rooted in context fragmentation. Solving it requires systems that can interpret behavior, adapt dynamically, and take actions on behalf of the user.

Consider a recent example: In one sales organization operating in the fast-moving AI category, the messaging shifted six times in nine months. The team couldn't afford to wait for formal certification cycles or LMS updates. Instead, they had to experiment in real time, adjusting content on the fly, refining based on rep feedback, and responding to market shifts week by week.

The challenge wasn't creating the content. It was getting it to the field with speed, structure, and context. Distribution lagged. Reinforcement was inconsistent. Traditional systems, built on APIs and asynchronous updates, simply couldn't keep up. The enablement architecture wasn't designed for this level of adaptability. No matter how strong the content or intent, it couldn't reach reps fast enough to make an impact.

📔 What We Mean by "Legacy Architecture"

Legacy architecture refers to systems built on older software principles, often modular, rules-based, and reliant on integrations between disconnected tools. These systems were effective for managing structured workflows in a more predictable pre-AI era.

The AI native world moves faster, processing signals that are constant, making decisions is dynamic, and its value comes from reasoning, not just surfacing data. Legacy systems were designed to deliver functionality rather than intelligence and weren't built to interpret this complexity in real time.

What We Mean by "Asynchronous Update Cycles"

Asynchronous update cycles refer to how data is passed between systems on a time delay. These are traditionally scheduled in batches or refresh intervals. In legacy environments, this is a common constraint.

For example, a CRM might sync activity from an email tool every fifteen minutes. But in a high-velocity sales cycle, those delays add up, causing reps to miss buying signals or act on stale information.

In an AI native system, updates are continuous, so the user gets a true reflection of what's happening now, not what happened twenty minutes ago.

📘 *What We Mean by "API Bridges"*

API bridges allow different systems to exchange data, like syncing activities between a CRM and a sales engagement platform. While APIs enable integration, traditional API bridges are often brittle; they depend on static formatting, token validity, and compatible field structures. Something as small as a key expiration or a schema change can silently break the flow.

These bridges were built to connect systems but not to understand or interpret what's being passed. They lack memory, reasoning, and shared context.

While APIs still play a role, they're often governed by an architectural layer like the Model Context Protocol (MCP), a shared protocol that allows AI models to retrieve data intelligently, maintain continuity, and enable reasoning across multiple systems and workflows.

This is what makes true orchestration possible—not just passing information but understanding its role in the broader loop of decisions, actions, and outcomes.

4.3 What's Needed: A Fundamentally Different Architecture

To move from reactive fixes to a fully orchestrated system, we must go beyond patchwork integrations and invest in a new architecture built for intelligence in motion. This fundamentally different foundation must be designed to unify data, workflow, and intelligence to offer reasoning and action at scale. It's this system architecture—not a feature or a dashboard—that ultimately enables the behavioral principles described earlier.

- *Agentic* systems act on behalf of the rep, not just suggest.
- *Embedded* workflows surface enablement in the tools reps already use.
- *Conversational* interfaces allow AI to interact naturally and explain itself.
- *Real-time* performance enables instant feedback, nudges, and adaptation.
- *Self-improving* systems learn from rep behavior to refine future action.

These aren't features—they're outcomes of a system designed for continuous, context-aware execution.

Drawing from the AI Native System Blueprint, five architectural foundations form the technical core of a system built to reason, act, and scale with intelligence.

Unified, Contextual Real-Time Data Layer

Traditional systems rely on batch updates and disconnected sources that fragment the customer experience and delay decisions. In contrast, an AI native system requires a data layer that not only captures data across CRM, email, meetings, chat, and more but does so in a way that preserves relationships, meaning, and intent.

This creates a dynamic 360-degree view of rep and customer activity—*not just as events, but as signals*—enabling high-velocity, coordinated decision-making across the organization. It's not about having more data; it's about having the right data with the right context exactly when it matters.

Reasoning Engine

A reasoning engine elevates the system from informational to intentional. It processes data in context, detecting patterns, interpreting behavior, and recommending next steps. Rather than simply stating that a deal is off track, it identifies why (e.g., low champion engagement or objection handling gaps) and prescribes remedies. This engine becomes more accurate and personalized as it learns from outcomes.

Agentic Workflow Layer

This is the action layer, the part of the system that doesn't just assist the rep but acts on their behalf. It responds to signals in real time, triggering follow-ups, sending reminders, surfacing relevant content, and even scheduling coaching, just as a great rep or manager would. This layer turns enablement into an intelligent copilot, one that overcomes mental load inertia, initiates motion, and keeps execution aligned without waiting to be told what to do.

Native Compute and Execution Engine

Enablement needs to move at the speed of customer conversations. That means insights can't sit in disparate systems or dashboards. They must become action, triggered instantly and reliably. A native compute and execution engine allows the system to do just that: process and execute actions directly within its own infrastructure without relying on external services, third-party syncs, or brittle API bridges.

But speed alone isn't what makes this essential. Native compute is what allows action to happen securely, contextually, and at scale. It ensures data governance, minimizes integration risk and enables seamless orchestration across the enablement flywheel. When paired with a unified, contextual data layer, native compute becomes the foundation for agentic systems—turning signal into motion with precision and trust.

Composable Interface

Interfaces shouldn't just be user friendly. They should be user ready. A **composable interface** adapts in real time to the role, context, and intent of the user, whether that's a rep working in Slack, a manager operating in CRM, or an AI agent executing tasks behind the scenes.

This means the system doesn't just display everything it knows. It displays only what's needed *right now.* A rep deep in a deal may see only the next best action and a "Send" button rather than a full playbook. A CRM layout might surface just the fields that matter at a given stage, removing clutter and guiding precision.

Composability transforms the interface from a static workspace into an intelligent decision layer, so enablement shows up where decisions are made, not buried behind logins, tabs, or irrelevant screens.

These architectural principles aren't theoretical. They are already beginning to take shape. Early signals include live CRM overlays, real-time coaching triggers, and AI copilots embedded directly into rep workflows.

DevRev offers one of the clearest architectural models for enabling AI native behavior. Its platform unifies product, customer, and GTM data to support real-time intelligence, contextual reasoning, and agentic workflows. While not purpose-built exclusively for sales enablement, DevRev's infrastructure demonstrates how

AI-authored summaries, embedded copilots, and workflow orchestration can operate natively and without being retrofitted onto legacy systems. Becoming truly AI native likely won't mean keeping every system as is. This shift will require rethinking the workspace itself— where intelligence is no longer a layer but the logic that drives every interaction. It reflects what's possible when intelligence is integrated directly into the operational backbone of go-to-market teams.

This is a glimpse into a future where systems don't just inform. They adapt, interpret, and respond. The flywheel is already turning, but to keep it going, we need systems that can understand context and take smart action, not simply provide more data.

📔 *What We Mean by "Mental Load Inertia"*

Mental load inertia refers to the drag that occurs when reps face too much cognitive overhead, usually stemming from too many systems, decisions, or unclear priorities. Even high-performing sellers can stall when the path forward isn't obvious. AI native systems can reduce this friction by anticipating needs and initiating action so reps stay in motion, not stuck in deliberation.

📙 What We Mean by "Data Governance"

Historically, data and security risks have been a major blocker to innovation in sales enablement. Teams were cautious about exposing sensitive customer and rep data across fragmented tools and third-party services. As a result, even when AI or automation was available, deployment was often limited to low-risk, low-impact areas. Native compute changes that equation. Because actions stay inside the governed system boundary, organizations can unlock real-time orchestration without compromising on control. Security isn't just a box to check; it becomes a catalyst for scale.

4.4 Organizational Shift: The System Beyond the Architecture

Even the best architecture will fall short if the organization doesn't evolve with it. AI native enablement isn't just a technical shift. It's an organizational one. The infrastructure may be capable of orchestration, but that's meaningless if teams are still operating from traditional assumptions and behaviors.

What's missing isn't just tooling but the ability to respond. To experiment. To adapt. It's the belief that action can precede certainty. That pilots matter more than polish. That feedback loops are inputs, not criticisms. That different teams might need different things, and that's not inefficiency. It's evolution.

We've seen teams invest in advanced AI tools, only to deploy them with static rollouts, top-down training models, and rigid launch cycles. In the end, those tools remain constrained with expensive technology trapped inside outdated workflows.

Even the most advanced orchestration engine won't create outcomes if the organization isn't designed to respond to its signals. Think of the AI native system like a GPS. It offers turn-by-turn guidance, but it's up to the driver to follow it, correct course, and trust the map.

To unlock the promise of AI native enablement, organizations need to evolve how they build, test, scale, and support change. This means shifting from internal alignment to field responsiveness. From uniformity to adaptability. From proving value before launch to proving it through use.

What follows are three mindset shifts that help organizations operationalize a system that's designed to respond—not just deliver—plus one structural shift that reimagines how enablement is embedded across the business.

Pilot for Impact, Don't Launch for Optics

In an AI native world, success won't come from big-bang rollouts. It requires a shift in mindset, from valuing scale and uniformity to embracing focus, iteration, and responsiveness.

This means shifting from "launch for everyone" to "pilot where it matters most." A program deployed to three reps is not incomplete. It's targeted. It allows teams to learn quickly, refine in context, and scale only when there's signal that it's working. This mindset prioritizes adaptability over optics.

It also means letting go of the idea that everyone needs the same thing at the same time. Some reps may self-select into deeper engagement; others may need a different path. That's not a failure of fairness but a sign of a system working as designed.

What this mindset shift looks like in action: Giving more opportunities, resources, and attention to reps who actively engage and want more rather than holding back for the sake of uniformity. Spending less time forcing adoption among reps with other priorities. Not all teams will adopt the same tools at the same time, and that's okay.

> This reflects the principle of design for action, not just information transfer, giving reps contextual, timely opportunities to apply learning in the flow of work rather than overwhelming them with static, one-size-fits-all rollouts.

Iterate, Don't Wait for Steady State

In a world where the pace of change outstrips certainty, experimentation isn't risky but responsible. Organizations must get comfortable with the idea that not everything needs to be perfect—or even universal—before it's released. This calls for a shift in mindset; enablement isn't a static function. It's an evolving product.

Like modern product teams, enablement organizations must begin to work in agile cycles, delivering in sprints, shipping MVPs, and treating feedback as a core input, not an interruption. This mindset values usability and iteration over volume and perfection. It assumes that learning happens in the field, not in isolation.

This shift also requires a change in expectations from both enablement and sales leadership. Sales leaders must let go of the assumption that what's launched needs to be fully formed, polished, or one-size-fits-all. Instead, they must embrace the idea that enablement is now closer to a product discipline: built in sprints, informed by feedback, and evolving in the field. Product, marketing, and enablement teams also need to stop optimizing for internal readiness and begin optimizing for field responsiveness. Success isn't about launching what's complete; it's about shipping what's useful and improving it through use. This mindset normalizes change, trusts iteration, and treats adaptation as a core competency, not a concession.

What this mindset shift looks like in action: Building iteration into the launch plan. Sharing what was learned from a pilot before expanding. Empowering managers and reps to cocreate future versions of enablement rather than waiting for HQ to finalize it. Operating on feedback cycles that prioritize real-world performance over internal opinion.

> This reinforces these principles: Enablement is a system, and rep development is owned by their manager. Like any system, its value compounds through real-time feedback and iteration. Managers play a critical role in this loop; they aren't just recipients of programs but active participants in shaping and evolving them. Empowering managers to iterate in the field is part of making the system truly flexible.

Choose for the Future, Not the Familiar

Legacy tools were built for a different era that was focused on static content, episodic training, and delayed insight. Today's AI native enablement requires platforms that are real-time, adaptive, and system-oriented. Yet many organizations default to familiar vendors or stitched-together stacks, hoping that incremental improvements will create transformational outcomes.

They won't. Putting AI on top of legacy architecture is like putting jet fuel in a Prius—it may run, but it was never built to fly.

To move forward, organizations will need to shift their mindset from comfort to capability. This means evaluating tools based on how well they orchestrate workflows, surface real-time insight, and integrate into daily execution, not how established they are in an analyst report.

It also means letting go of the idea that there's a single stack or blueprint for enablement. The right system might not look like what came before. It might come from newer vendors, it might be composable, and it might require redefining how teams work across RevOps, product, and sales.

What this mindset shift looks like in action: Asking whether a system is architected to evolve with your vision, not just whether it performs a function today. Can the current architecture support what you need tomorrow, or is it fundamentally limited by design? Evaluating platforms based not only on how they report or integrate but on whether they can reason, adapt, and grow into the full enablement system you're building. Prioritizing vendors who support orchestration and intelligence, not just functional execution in isolated workflows.

> True system thinking requires us to be future-facing, not only in what we say but in what we choose to build with.

Rethink Enablement as a Shared System, Not a Standalone Team

The promise of AI native enablement can't be unlocked by sales alone. As workflows become more interconnected and intelligence flows across functions, enablement must evolve from a siloed support function into a distributed capability embedded within every GTM function.

This might call for a new type of organizational structure where each department has a dedicated enablement role focused on GTM impact. In product marketing, this could be someone who translates feature launches into buyer narratives and outbound plays. In customer success, a role might focus on surfacing upsell opportunities, capturing expansion stories, and relaying voice-of-customer insights back into training. In product, a liaison could help teams interpret how technical updates impact revenue, account expansion, or usage trends.

These GTM-facing roles work in parallel to the core sales enablement team, ensuring each department is plugged into the field—not just via handoffs but through shared accountability. They also help transform insight into action, bridging between functionally owned systems and the centralized enablement loop.

What this mindset shift looks like in action: Each function contributes to a unified enablement roadmap with embedded stakeholders ensuring alignment between their team's priorities and field needs. These roles participate in feedback loops, help shape programs in response to real-world signals, and ensure that enablement stays contextual, current, and connected across silos.

> This shift reinforces a central truth: AI native enablement isn't a departmental initiative. It's the operating system for go-to-market success.

5

Sales Enablement in the AI Native World

Sales enablement has always been about empowering sellers to succeed, but the systems around them have struggled to keep up. We've seen waves of innovation, from playbooks and LMSs to content libraries and call coaching tools. But now, the world has changed. The workflows are faster. The customers are savvier. And the margin for wasted motion is razor thin.

Sales enablement is no longer about delivering information. It's about creating motion. This isn't just a tooling problem; it's a cultural one. And it requires a complete rethinking of how we structure teams, build systems, and respond to signals.

In an AI native world, the difference between knowing and executing comes down to system design, organizational mindset, and the ability to adapt in real time.

We've explored the foundational principles of great enablement, unpacked how to measure progress, reimagined the flywheel as a dynamic AI native system, and outlined the architectural and organizational shifts required to make it real. This isn't a future state. It's already underway.

Leading the System Change

Sales enablement is no longer a toolkit. It's a platform. And platforms aren't built through assets or isolated training sessions. They are built through architecture, systems thinking, and leadership. For years, enablement has responded to business needs with episodic programs: onboarding tracks, pitch decks, certification paths. But the pace and complexity of modern selling have outgrown that model. The workflows are faster. The stakes are higher. And the systems supporting the field can no longer afford to lag behind it.

Throughout this book, we've explored what great enablement looks like when it's built with intention: how it's structured, how it's measured, and how it evolves. But more than a playbook, this is a provocation to move beyond incremental updates and reimagine enablement as a continuous system of learning, execution, and adaptation. That shift demands more than just new tooling. It calls for new choices: to architect for orchestration, connecting content, coaching, data, and analytics into one dynamic loop; to design programs like products—modular, user-tested, and field-driven; and to lead through shared ownership, ensuring enablement isn't delivered from the sidelines but embedded in the day-to-day rhythm of the business.

This transformation doesn't require a full-scale rebuild from day one. It begins by examining the flywheel already in place. Where are reps stalling? Where is content going unused? Where are insights failing to translate into action? These moments aren't just signs of friction. They're signals. And each one offers a chance to ask a new kind of question: What would it take for the system—not the seller—to solve this?

What's broken isn't motivation. It's architecture. And what's missing isn't more content or compliance but a system designed to meet people where they are. The future of enablement isn't defined by more programs. It's shaped by better systems that reason across context, take action at the moment of need, and evolve with every interaction. When those systems are designed with clarity, coaching, and contextual signals at the core, something deeper emerges: trust.

Trust changes everything. When reps trust the system around them—because it works, because it helps, because it learns—they don't just adopt it. They grow through it. And that trust doesn't come from tools alone. It comes from systems, carefully designed, continuously refined, and built with people in mind.

The Final Word

This book is about enablement, but it's also about leadership.

About building systems that reflect what we believe about performance, progress, and people.

We don't have to choose between rigor and relevance. Between humans and machines.

We just have to build better systems—and trust them enough to carry us forward.

The architecture is possible. The signals are already here.

The only question left is this:

Will you be the one to lead the system change before it leaves you behind?

Enablement isn't a function. It's a platform for action. Let's build it together.

Epilogue

I didn't set out to write a book. I just kept running into the same pattern, across companies, across teams, across time. Sales enablement was being asked to drive behavior change without the systems or alignment to support it.

Over the past decade, I've worked inside high-growth startups and global go-to-market organizations, scaling enablement programs for teams navigating complexity, constant change, and conflicting priorities. Again and again, I saw reps struggling. Not because they lacked capability, but because the systems around them weren't built to support motion.

Then came AI.

And with it, a flood of new expectations. That content would become personalized. That coaching would somehow scale itself. That reps would become instantly productive, insight-driven, and efficient. The excitement was real—but so was the confusion. Underneath all the new tools, the same old problems remained.

This book wasn't written to explain AI. It was written to recenter enablement around what's always been true:

> People don't change because they're told what to do.

They change when systems support their behavior, when managers reinforce the message, and when the organization treats enablement as everyone's responsibility, not just one team's job.

That's why the first half of this book focused on the foundations—the principles of enablement that hold true in any context. The second half explored what becomes possible when those principles are embedded into architecture, tools, and intelligent workflows.

If there's one idea I hope stays with you, it's this:

- Enablement isn't about keeping up. It's about building the system that helps others move forward.
- The human truths haven't changed. The technology finally gives us a chance to deliver on them, but at scale.

Now the work begins.

EXHIBIT A

SDR Development Plan

Skill	Definition	What Good Looks like	Lagging Indicator
Account Research	Uncover and continuously monitor a company's business objectives, strategic initiatives, and activity signals to identify relevant use cases and align them to DevRev capabilities.	• Gathers insights from public sources (e.g., blogs, product updates, earnings calls) to understand the company's strategic priorities • Actively monitors changes in company behavior or signals (e.g., hiring, website visits, product activity) using available tools • Synthesizes new and existing information to keep use case hypotheses fresh and engagement efforts timely	Account or opportunity score (based on fields)

Skill	Definition	What Good Looks like	Lagging Indicator
Organizational Mapping	Identify and map out individuals across functions and levels within a target account to understand the organizational structure and uncover potential sources of insight aligned to company goals.	• Identifies individuals across relevant departments (e.g., support, product, engineering, operations), not just senior leaders • Maps out functional hierarchies to understand reporting lines, team structures, and influence paths • Prioritizes individuals based on their likely proximity to strategic initiatives or workflows relevant to DevRev use cases	Number of contacts tied to each account

Skill	Definition	What Good Looks like	Lagging Indicator
Communication and Messaging	Clearly and credibly communicate relevant insights, hypotheses, and value propositions across written and verbal channels, tailored to the recipient's role and business context.	• Writes concise, creative messages that reflect account-specific context and align to the recipient's role • Delivers confident, relevant messaging in live conversations, effectively articulating DevRev's point of view, product value, and how we uniquely address customer challenges • Responds to objections or signals in real time with empathy, curiosity, and control, avoiding reactive or rigid behavior	Response rates

Skill	Definition	What Good Looks like	Lagging Indicator
Stakeholder Engagement	Engage multiple stakeholders through thoughtful, ongoing outreach to uncover context, build familiarity, and surface insights that reveal opportunities for deeper exploration.	• Engages relevant individuals across levels and functions with consistent, value-based outreach, viewing engagement as a multi-touch, relationship-building effort • Builds trust by demonstrating curiosity, relevance, and a clear understanding of the account's goals and DevRev's potential fit • Navigates conversations with intent, uncovering insights, validating or refining the use case hypothesis, and creating strategic access for deeper discovery and multithreading	Number of contacts at an opportunity

Skill	Definition	What Good Looks like	Lagging Indicator
Discovery	Guide conversations with genuine curiosity, asking layered, thoughtful questions that peel back the onion to uncover deeper context, challenges, and alignment to DevRev's value and the MEDDPICC framework.	• Asks hypothesis-driven questions that guide the conversation toward relevant areas of pain or opportunity • Uses follow-up and second-layer questions to dig deeper and clarify stakeholder context, goals, or blockers • Listens for patterns, blockers, or internal friction that signal where DevRev could create leverage or improve outcomes	MEDDPICC score

Skill	Definition	What Good Looks like	Lagging Indicator
Systems and Tools	Demonstrates curiosity, enthusiasm, and adaptability when adopting new tools and technologies, using them regularly to enhance performance across research, outreach, stakeholder engagement, and discovery.	• Embraces new technology (e.g., DevRev, ChatGPT, 6sense, Outreach, Slack) as a natural part of the daily workflow • Thoughtfully incorporates tools into day-to-day execution, using them to accelerate account research, streamline outreach, and improve call prep • Iterates on workflows and shares tooling best practices with peers to help level up the broader team	Tooling score

Skill	Definition	What Good Looks like	Lagging Indicator
Operational Excellence	Demonstrates the discipline, consistency, and ownership needed to execute at a high level, including meeting prep, time management, data hygiene, and performance self-inspection.	• Prepares thoroughly for meetings with AEs and prospects, manages time effectively, and maintains consistent execution across accounts • Maintains clean, complete CRM data in DevRev to ensure the entire organization—including AI, support, and product—can operate with accurate context • Regularly inspects personal performance data to identify what's working, adjust inputs, and drive continuous improvement	Hits all weekly activity targets (meetings and emails)
Skill	For each of the skills above, make as based on a rating (1-5)	What were the things you did or are going to do next week to improve this?	Completion Assessment

EXHIBIT B

Market Signals—Vendor Tools Reflecting the Shift

Capability Area	Vendors	What They're Trying
Coaching and Role-play	Gong, SalesMagic, AdamX, PepSales, Enterprise Chai	Embedding call-based and pre-call AI coaching; synthetic role-play simulations
Enrichment	ZoomInfo, Clay, Clearbit	Expanding data freshness and reach with AI but still tied to batch enrichment models
Sequencing and Engagement	Lavender, Regie.ai, Klenty, Sprout.ai	Moving from persona-based sequences to signal-based, intent-driven engagement flows

Workflow Orchestration	UnifyGTM, GTM Buddy, Scratchpad	Triggering in-context nudges and content based on rep actions or deal stage
Analytics and Insight	Revvolution.ai, TigerEye, InsightSquared, Clari	Providing dynamic insights tied to pipeline velocity, rep behavior, and forecast accuracy; enabling real-time deal health assessments and pipeline visibility across teams
Sales Content and Guidance	Highspot, Seismic, Enable.us, Thread	Delivering personalized, searchable content in the flow of work with AI curation
Product-Led Enablement	Productboard, Pendo, LaunchNotes	Turning product usage and feedback into enablement triggers and storytelling
Manager Enablement	SecondNature, Mindtickle, Saleshood	Delivering personalized coaching plans and cohort-led reinforcement from managers
Embedded Enablement Tools	Salesloft, Outreach, Docket.io	Integrating guidance into daily tools—email, calendars, meetings—for just-in-time delivery

EXHIBIT C

AI Native Flywheel Readiness Checklist

Use this to gauge how AI-ready each pillar of the flywheel from Section 3 is today and pinpoint the highest-leverage moves.

Pick one or two of them to focus on each quarter and make a plan around how you'll get there.

1 | Content—Ships Itself

- How modular—and AI-addressable—is our content? Can a rep (or AI agent) grab a single "brick" without sifting through a forty-page deck?
- How well is content tailored to each delivery mode? Does Slack get a 150-word snippet while

the AI agent receives a structured prompt, or are we just chopping slides and hoping?

- How connected is our content performance data? Does every asset report usage and outcomes to a shared store so AI can learn across the library, or does each asset sit in its own silo with disjointed metrics?

2 | Programs—Turn Knowledge into Muscle Memory

- How does onboarding get reps into action? Do new hires start real prospecting tasks on day one—guided by AI prompts—or wait until bootcamp graduation to touch live work?
- How are ongoing skills paced? Does data plus AI feed each rep the next module based on their progress, or does everyone follow the same weekly schedule?
- How does manager coaching plug in? Do leaders sharpen their coaching skills by practicing with AI-simulated conversations before the one-on-one so feedback lands, or do they still wing it live?

3 | Sales AI Agent—Works for Reps

- How many tabs does a rep open per deal? One side-pane agent or five stand-alone point tools?
- Can the agent act on the rep's behalf? Does it draft follow-ups, log notes, and trigger next steps? Are high-risk opportunities flagged early with a clear, prioritized next-best-action list, or does it just add information that increases mental load?
- How does the agent surface deal context without extra effort? Does it auto-package key risks and milestones for the rep, giving managers instant, transparent insight instead of forcing reps to write long updates or rely on a black box summary?

4 | Analytics—Closes the Loop in Real Time

- How rich is your streaming data context? Does the system send raw events with no meaning or stream events wrapped in an ontology (knowledge) graph so AI sees the full story in real time?

- How prescriptive is the system once it spots risk? Does the AI connect behaviors to the leading indicators that drive performance and surface the *specific* change needed to turn the deal around, or does it just predict bad news?

- How actionable—and role aware—is each insight? Can users drill from a high-level card? Does each role get the specific data they need—and trigger a tailored next step—or does everyone get a generic chart that just adds noise?

How to Use This

1. **Copy these prompts into your next enablement or RevOps meeting.**

2. **Rate each answer:**
   - ◉ we nail it
   - ◯ room to improve
   - ○ gap

Acknowledgments

Writing a book is never a solo effort, and I am deeply grateful to the many people who made this one possible.

First, thank you to the team at **Amplify Publishing**, especially for your belief in this project and for helping bring clarity, structure, and polish to my vision. Your partnership and professionalism made every step feel possible.

I am deeply grateful to **Dheeraj Pandey**, who sparked this journey. It was your simple but powerful question— *"What does good look like for sales enablement?"*—that planted the seed for this book. Your vision for AI created the ideal backdrop for the thinking that followed.

Manoj Agarwal constantly challenged me to think more critically and creatively about how AI can elevate sales. Your curiosity and candor have pushed my thinking forward in ways that show up throughout these pages.

Elay Cohen, thank you for your generous feedback, thoughtful edits, and unwavering support. Your perspective sharpened the thinking and elevated the clarity of this book. I'm grateful for your time, care, and the wisdom you bring from years of building and scaling enablement teams.

Luca Lazzaron gave me what felt like an MBA in sales. The clarity, discipline, and rigor I learned under your leadership shaped the foundations of how I lead today. Much of this book's core principles around sales enablement were developed during my time with you.

The guests of the *State of the AI Union* podcast stretched my thinking and often landed directly on these pages. Thank you for being generous with your time and ideas.

To **Jo and Mona,** my sisters from other misters— thank you for always believing in me, for understanding both my tech brain and my heart, and for encouraging me not just through this book, but throughout my whole adult life.

To my children—**Jadon, Hudson, Ellie, Atalia, and Jesse**—thank you for your patience, for grounding me in what's real, and for being my daily reminder that progress is rarely linear, but always worth it.

To my partner, **Chef Charlie Parker**—thank you for keeping me fed (literally!) while I chased down every last sentence. Your quiet gift was giving me exactly the space I needed through the many late nights and long weekends it took to bring this to completion.

Above all, I am grateful to God for His faithfulness, provision, and grace throughout this journey—not just in writing this book, but in every season that led here.

This book is for everyone working to build something better—in their team, their company, and themselves.

About the Author

Laura Fu is a global go-to-market leader and sales enablement strategist who has built high-performing revenue teams and scaled operations across every stage of growth.

With nearly two decades of experience spanning venture-backed startups and public companies like Sprinklr, Kong, Olo, and Gigya, Laura has architected go-to-market systems that drive clarity, accountability, and sustained performance. At Sprinklr, she played a pivotal role in scaling international operations and sales enablement, helping new markets achieve over 100 percent of booking goals while implementing global programs that accelerated rep ramp and pipeline productivity. At Kong and Olo, she led GTM transformation efforts—rebuilding sales rhythms, territory models, and onboarding programs to reduce time-to-performance and improve operational visibility for leadership.

Now leading Revenue Strategy and Operations at DevRev, Laura is at the forefront of applying AI to modern sales strategy and execution. Her focus: exploring how AI can support sales organizations—from improving pipeline coverage and forecasting visibility to enabling faster execution across the GTM motion. As AI reshapes how technology is built, sold, and supported, Laura's work centers on designing adaptive systems that keep pace with innovation while elevating human potential.

Her enablement philosophy blends empathy for the sales craft with a builder's mindset and a chef's sense of flow and precision. (Yes—she's also a classically trained chef, which shows in her creativity and execution under pressure.) Whether onboarding a new rep or overhauling a go-to-market strategy, Laura brings a rare combination of operational rigor and human-centered design.

She is also the creator and host of *The State of the AI Union*, a podcast that explores how AI is transforming product, GTM, and customer experience—through the eyes of operators, founders, and builders.

Based in Palo Alto by way of Singapore, Laura brings a global perspective to leadership, learning, and scale. She's also a proud mom of four, balancing the chaos of family life with the rigor of revenue strategy—proof that systems thinking works both at work and at home. *Designing for Excellence* is her first book—a practical, forward-looking guide to building sales teams that thrive in a world defined by continuous change.